Right now a very select group of people learn the wisdom, knowledge, importance and prominence of **Re**ology—embracing internal reality and minimizing the role of external reality as a life shaper. And a very small, almost immeasurable percentage of the population have **Re**Speak as a tool for evolved thinking and happier living. It is almost unimaginable to think how **Re**ology and its teachings can alter the way we perceive, interact and connect with one another. And how happiness can proliferate. When I think of how **Re**ologic (a new word) principles can reshape the course of a child's life and how that may resonate in adulthood, I get goose bumps.

Steve Wedeen, Principal at VWK, Albuquerque, New Mexico

§

Attending the **Re**ology retreat in such an amazing setting . . . sleeping with elk, consuming only fabulous healthy food, meditating, laughing, and relating with the other participants chiseled away at the crust that had grown over me for the past many years. I experienced spiritual and emotional connections that broke down that distant, sluggish and depressed soul that was inside me.

I was able to gift my mind, body and soul with radiance and a new perspective so that I am finally awake again. I am now taking ownership as to how I am going to work through my relationship hiccups, refocus on parenting excellence and address ongoing work challenges.

Make no mistake, this was one of the most challenging things I have ever done but super rewarding.

Michael Obraitis, Entrepreneur, Fort Lauderdale, Florida

As a cancer survivor, the **Re**ology retreat I attended and the practice of using **Re**Speak facilitated my healing process and personal growth in the most challenging moments that life presents.

Cecilia Biglieri, Mental Health Counselor,
Albuquerque, New Mexico

§

Reology is a revolutionary approach to dealing with the age-old challenge of effectively communicating with others. This book has positively transformed my practice of medicine by deepening my understanding of successful patient-doctor dynamics and how to optimize this in successful treatment outcomes. I highly recommend this book for anyone desiring a radical shift in communication and learning how to take responsibility for their life.

Michael Amster, M.D., Medical Director,
Northbay Center for Pain Management, Davis, California

§

Learning to use **Re**Speak has enabled me to interact with myself and others in much more positive and constructive ways. Using these skills, my husband and I continue to transform our marriage—after twenty years of being together—in ways I would not have thought possible.

Elyn Aviva, Ph.D., M.Div., Spain

§

As a Yoga teacher and educator in corporate America, I have experienced incredible value in learning ReSpeak. I'm convinced that if teachers and coaches learn to speak in this new way, they're going to be much more effective.

Lars Strong, Educator, Santa Fe, New Mexico

With **Re**ology, and Jake's guidance, I have grown and expanded myself in ways I never could have imagined. These skills, that I continue to learn and master, have proved to be invaluable in creating successful intimate relationships. In my profession as a therapist, I have found **Re**Speak to be an amazing tool in helping clients quickly shift from victimizing themselves to taking personal responsibility...

Mary Eloisa, Licensed Clinical Mental Health Counselor, British Columbia, Canada

§

I decided upon arrival at the **Re**ology retreat that I wanted to look at my relationship with my nine-year-old daughter. I have struggled with this relationship since she was about a year and have worked with a therapist extensively to help better my interactions with her. Since attending the retreat, I have been amazed at the HUGE shift I had around dealing with her and my lack of patience and acceptance of this little person in my life. This is something I haven't been able to do in eight years of therapy.

Lacey Clark, Mother, Seattle, Washington

§

Reology presents a new language, **Re**Speak, making a unique contribution to the field of personal development—possibly the most significant advancement in human consciousness since the days of Freud. Use the simple and profound language tools in this book and you will soon discover a perspective that transforms your internal life and relationships in remarkable and unexpected ways.

Mike Bundrant, Publisher of Healthy Times and radio talk show host of Mental Health Exposed, Murrieta, California

ReRight Your Life

An Introduction to Reology

Jake Eagle

WORLD WISE PRESS
40 RIVER VALLEY ROAD
SANTA FE, NEW MEXICO
87506

978-0-9841362-2-3   Paperback
978-0-9841362-3-0   ePub
978-0-9841362-4-7   Hardcover

Library of Congress Cataloging-in-Publication Data
Eagle, Jake
ReRight Your Life, An Introduction To **Re**ology
p. cm
q. Includes bibliographical references
r.
ISBN 978-0-9841362-2-3 (paperback: 1 color text)
I. Self Help, Personal Growth, Psychology, Spirituality

2013934738

To my wife and partner

—Hannah Eagle—

Beauty framed by impermanence

Acknowledgments

I want to thank the people who have come to me for therapy and counseling over the past twenty years—as well as people who have attended our workshops. I inspire myself working with you—filling my life with rich and meaningful interactions.

§

Also, I want to thank the following individuals for reading my manuscript and providing thoughtful contributions:

Rick Halpern · Kelly Kindig · Michelle Faucher
Dixie Foley · Mike Bundrant · Katie Bell
Pat Wartell · Talitha Benjamin · Stephen Landau
Kimber Shining Star · Aleza Stirling
David MacKenzie · Susan Perkins
Shayla Wright · Ralph Huber · Jan Harrow
Jill Bailin

§

In addition to witnessing my parent's loving relationship, I've been fortunate to have wise mentors in my life. In this book I share some details about the profound consequences of my relationship with John Weir. I also want to acknowledge the generosity of Nelson Zink, and the significance of his guidance.

§

Cover design by Steve Wedeen/VWK Albuquerque, NM:
www.vwk2.com
Interior photography by David MacKenzie:
www.wondereveryday.com

NOTE TO MY READERS

The first edition of this book was originally published in 2010 as, *Speak Love Not War, An Introduction To Green Psychology.* In 2013 I'm releasing the second edition. Although a great deal of the content remains the same as the first edition, the important discoveries I've made—along with my wife Hannah— in the past three years created an imperative for me to write this new version.

"Green Psychology" represented the body of work that we'd spent so many years developing. The name was intended to emphasize the importance of growth, and also, sustainability in our relationships. Personal growth and sustainable relationships remain the focus of our work, but as our understanding has evolved, we've come to believe that our new name—being introduced in this book—will help advance our work in the world.

Our new name is based on our discovery of two letters, maybe the most important two letters in the English language: RE. Because of the power of RE, which you will learn about in this book, we have renamed the body of work we teach. It is now called **Re**ology. Our emphasis on words that begin with RE will become clear to you as you read this book. We believe that in time, every time you use a word that begins with RE, you will simultaneously become aware that you have a choice—a choice to **Re**do yourself and **Re**-Right yourself.

Table of Contents

Introduction

I want to offer you a gift. The gift is a way of living, an actual practice that fosters peaceful coexistence, first with yourself, then with others: your partner, your parents, your children, your siblings.

In this book, my focus is on my brother. A few months ago he was diagnosed with an inoperable brain tumor. I cannot ignore the fierce urgency of this moment. He and I may not have tomorrow.

For the past ten years I've been writing a book, sort of a user-friendly textbook intended to explain human development and behavior. But while my head was down, diligently writing, life happened and I didn't see it coming. It took a family crisis for me to see that I wasn't applying the wisdom of my own book to my relationship with my brother. When he became seriously ill, I threw my book away. Because of my brother's illness, I grew impatient with myself; time became my editor. I began to ask myself some challenging questions.

Why wasn't I practicing with my brother what I believed would have allowed us to connect? Why had it taken a crisis for me to wake up in relation to him? Why had I held back for so long? As a result of these questions a new conversation was born. My brother became my muse and a completely different book emerged, the one you hold in your hands.

These pages offer words that are precious to me and prescient for all of us. At times on this journey I screamed into the void of death and heard nothing come back. I tortured myself with the silence. I'm compelled to share my experience with others so they may benefit. This is a heartfelt expression and exploration of ideas I've developed over many years.

These ideas are not just to be read; they accrue value only when they are practiced. In practicing them I learned more about life and death, about renewal and regret, and about the price of procrastination.

Adopting this practice wakes up the adult in us and we become fully responsible for how we conduct ourselves. No excuses. No hiding behind our limitations or our wounded childhoods. No defending ourselves when our actions don't match our intentions. No blaming others. We all have limitations; this way of living asks us to take responsibility for our limitations. We all have wounds; this way of living asks us to heal our wounds. We have all behaved in ways that are not aligned with our intentions; this way of living asks us to realign with our intentions, right now. We have all been blamed and we have blamed; this way of living asks us to let go of our need to be right, which is the origin of blame.

This practice is not so much about change as it is about growth. So often we chase after a "better life." We work hard to bring about change, exhausting ourselves in the process. And often the change doesn't last. The problem with such an approach is that it presupposes something is wrong. It says that we are broken or flawed. That we need to be fixed. This creates enormous pressure.

I want to share with you a gentle way of living, deeply rooted in our natural desire to grow and mature. It relies on our innate ability to do so. It is not exhausting. It is stimulating and invigorating. At its essence this practice addresses what I perceive to be our deepest existential challenges:

- We resist uncertainty. Yet uncertainty is the source of our creativity and freedom.

- We deny impermanence. Yet impermanence is what makes life precious and potent.

- We evade being in the present. Yet the present is the source of our power.

- We defend our Identity. Yet our Identity doesn't need defending because it's a renewable mental construct.

- We avoid taking radical responsibility for ourselves. Yet the greater the responsibility we take, the more fully alive we become.

When we resist, deny, evade, defend, or avoid ourselves, we confuse ourselves and we suffer. We can transform our suffering and that's what this book is about. It is an actual practice that offers a more graceful way to live.

I refer to it as **Re**ology, which is the art and science of **re**doing our lives. When we practice **Re**ology—and it is an actual practice—we shift away from blame and move toward taking greater personal responsibility, which produces vastly different results in our lives. Reology provides a set of tools that allows us to **re**view and **re**interpret our past and present experiences through a new prism. When we do this, we will see things differently—we will see *ourselves* differently—we will **re**new ourselves by living according to our mature values, and we will create emotional footprints that we are proud to leave behind.

I invite you to step forward, beginning a journey that will stimulate your growth and reflect your health. This is an invitation for you to open, to deeply explore, and to expand your entire Identity. If you want to pursue this way of living, I encourage you to begin the journey with a companion, a partner or friend. For although we alone are responsible for ourselves, we live our lives with others—synergistically and interactively—using reflections of ourselves to guide and shape our growth. We find our reflections in every thing and every person we encounter. Can you imagine living your life so that every person you encounter reflects your growth, health and beauty? Can you imagine rising above the need to be right with your siblings, parents, peers, and life partners? Can you imagine treating people's differences with dignity? Can you imagine retaining your sense of self-worth even during times when others don't see your value?

All of this is possible.

If we begin with ourselves, overcoming our fear of judgment, stopping even the subtlest forms of violence, revealing our uniqueness, and taking radical responsibility, we will proliferate peace in our lives.

Entering an Unknown World

I am the youngest of three siblings. My brother Tom was the firstborn, then my sister Lizabeth, and then me. Tom didn't have much to do with me for the first ten or twelve years of my life. He always seemed very preoccupied with himself and pretty much ignored me until I was a teenager. Even then we weren't close; we were competitive. It was probably mostly me who was competing…he was just doing his own thing, which he usually did very well. He played sports and so did I. He was four years older and that gave him quite an advantage when it came to athletics. But even as our age difference became less of a factor, he outperformed me because he was a tougher competitor.

We tried to be friends and we also tried to be business partners at different times in our lives. When I was in college, we bought a one-third interest in an old mill, which we planned to convert into a restaurant. Once, he came to live with me to help me build my house. It's as if we wanted to connect in some meaningful way, but under the surface, there was tension.

I don't know what our relationship was like for him. I seldom felt seen or heard or appreciated, except for times when he was in crisis, like when he broke up with his girlfriend and he needed a friend, a counselor, someone he could count on.

As I matured, Tom disapproved of many of the actions I took. He thought my need to pull back from our parents was hurtful to them and he wasn't enthusiastic about my first marriage or, interestingly, my divorce seven years later.

I eventually moved away from New England to New Mexico and after that, our paths separated. I became a psychotherapist, and he continued in the world of business and venture capital. I remarried and was very happy. My sense is that Tom wasn't. Although he was a good provider for his family and a remarkably loyal son, he wanted something he didn't have. He wanted to hit a home run but his life was based on what he perceived to be a series of singles and doubles.

Slowly, over about a decade—during which we didn't have a lot to do with one another—Tom started to appreciate the life I created for myself. He sometimes made comments to let me know he thought I'd done well, made good decisions…and between the lines I thought he was saying, "I respect you." Although I was still competing with him, as we aged the tension relaxed. Our conversations were lighter, more frequent, and friendlier. We were allies in our concern for our aging parents. We still weren't close, but we weren't pushing against one another.

Then in the winter of 2007, Tom flew to New Mexico to be with me on my birthday. This was highly unusual. I can't remember the last time we were together on my birthday. He didn't feel well during his visit. He complained of a headache. We all just assumed it was the altitude. Santa Fe sits at seven thousand feet —high desert—and some people require days to adjust to the thinner air.

That was the first time Tom had seen the new home Hannah and I had spent the previous year building. We had only just recently moved in. Tom pointed out places where he thought we should have put more lighting, and had ideas about how we could remotely control the stereo system. As always, he had wonderful suggestions about how to spend money—in this case, our money. I only found out after his visit, when I was talking with our mother, that he really loved our new home.

The time we spent together during that visit had felt softer to me. Tom expressed interest in my life, my work, and my plans. This was unfamiliar, but welcome. We talked a good deal about his work and his aspirations. The three of us, Tom, Hannah and I, went for walks, shared meals and watched movies. It was a sweet way to spend my birthday.

Two months later Hannah and I flew to California to visit my parents, my sister, and her son. Tom decided to join all of us. It was the first time our family—my parents and the three siblings —had been together in probably fifteen years. Tom went out of his way to make that possible. Once again, though, he showed up not feeling well. He had a headache and was nauseated. He said he thought it was food poisoning.

On the weekend we all went to the beach in Carpenteria. Tom continued to feel lousy, but he managed to go swimming in the cold water of a California winter. We took some family photos, had a picnic, and went for walks on the beach.

Tom and I enjoyed more conversation, and just like two kids, we shared our enthusiasm about his new MacBook Air computer. High-tech gadgets were always a source of mutual excitement for us. I just wish he'd felt better so that he could have enjoyed our rare family reunion.

When Tom headed back to Maine we were concerned, wondering if he was well enough to travel. He wasn't. He was seriously ill. Within a month he was diagnosed with an inoperable brain tumor.

In hindsight I've wondered about those visits, his opening, his curiosity, his unusual desire to connect. Had he sensed on some level that there was a crisis looming that was about to shake up his world? And I have asked myself why it took a crisis for us to connect. I wondered if his crisis would be a chance for us to relate with one another in a new way. Where would we begin? How far could we go?

Even with the serious threat of his illness, we didn't abandon our caution. We didn't run toward one another. There was still a barrier. But we did reach out and seek new ways to connect.

What follows is a compilation of various conversations, from Tom's first visit to our home—before anyone knew he was ill— to our time together in California, chats on the phone, emails, and conversations in the hospital. There are also conversations that occurred only in my mind.

Many of our conversations were driven by Tom's desire to learn about me and my life. He seemed deeply curious to understand the work that Hannah and I were doing in the world—we were teaching Reology seminars around the country and in other countries. He wanted to know what Reology was and if it might help him deal with the challenges he was facing.

I have taken the liberty of altering the timing and content of our conversations. I have done so in the hope of creating a clear presentation of Reology for the reader.

CHAPTER 1

Stepping Out of Your Conceptual Straitjacket

It was a beautiful morning to sit out on the porch, warmed by the early morning sun. We talked with each other as we never had before that day. I kept wondering why Tom was so interested in me and my work, but his curiosity seemed completely genuine.

Tom: Tell me about your book. Every time I ask you what you're doing you say, "Working on my book." Is it done yet? Do you have a publisher?

Jake: Nope, still looking for a publisher. You want to read it?

Tom: How long is it? And—

Jake: …Four hundred pages.

Tom: What's the title?

Jake: **Re**Right (r-i-g-h-t) Your Life, An Introduction to **Re**ology.

Tom: Really?

Jake: Yes. **Re**ology is a new psychological model. It offers an alternative, a healthier way for people to relate to themselves and to other people. It's a way to **re**place conflict with connection.

Tom: How about the Cliff Notes?

Jake: No Cliff Notes but I can summarize.

Tom: Perfect.

Jake: Have you heard of Martin Heidegger? Do you know who he was?

Tom: The philosopher. I learned about him from Will Miller when I was at UVM, probably the same place you learned about him.

Jake: I haven't thought of Will for years. You're right, he was my philosophy professor, but that's not when I learned about Heidegger. Did you know that he said, "Something will reveal itself to us only if we do not attempt to coerce it into one of our ready-made conceptual straitjackets." I love that line.

Tom: Will said that?

Jake: No, Heidegger. And that's what **Re**ology is about, encouraging people to take off their straitjackets, to **re**veal themselves as the phenomenon that they are.

Tom: Not every one is phenomenal.

Jake: Maybe not when you use the word as an adjective. But the Greek definition of the word "phenomenon" was "that which reveals itself." We can all **re**veal ourselves, but often we don't. We hide, we hold back. And as a result we don't live phenomenal lives.

Tom: And that's what you help people do?

Jake: Yes, but I don't talk about being phenomenal because it sounds kind of grandiose. I talk about being healthy. I don't just mean physical health, but mental, emotional and spiritual health. I think of them as being interconnected.

Tom: But your focus is on the emotional and mental areas.

Jake: I try not to view them as separate, but yes, my focus is primarily on the mental and emotional areas, and spiritual—all of which influence our physical wellbeing.

Tom: How do you measure mental and emotional health?

Jake: The healthier we are, the more appropriately we respond to the world. As we become healthier we develop a wider range of behaviors and the emotional maturity to determine what responses are appropriate in any given situation. Because of this, healthier people tend to be happy or satisfied even though we live in an imperfect world. Heidegger didn't use the word "health," but he spoke of a state of being in which we focus less on how things are in the world, and focus more on the miracle of being, allowing ourselves to marvel that things are, that we are.

Tom: What about people who aren't healthy?

Jake: Let's not make it binary. There are varying degrees of health. The less healthy, the less appropriate our responses. If our ideas about ourselves or the world are distorted, it's very hard to know what's appropriate. We may respond to our lover as if she were our mother. We may respond to our child as if she were an adult. Or as adults, we may respond to situations in life as if we're still children. The more distorted our thinking, the more inappropriate and extreme our behaviors become.

Tom: Like what?

Jake: Extreme behaviors include trying to dominate and control people. Or acting as if we're powerless and victimized by other people. Distorted thinking leads to distorted behaviors, which show up in a variety of ways. And they all cause some confusion, because they aren't appropriate for what's going on in this moment.

There were times, a few years ago, when I would arrive home and expect Hannah to come down from her office and greet me, regardless of what she was doing. When she did greet me, I expected her to read my mind, to know how I was feeling. If I needed a particular kind of attention, I expected her to know what that was and—this is embarrassing—to take care of my needs. The reason I had this expectation is...

Tom: The reason you had that expectation is because that's exactly what Mom used to do for you when you were a kid.

Jake: Exactly. I'd come home and Mom would greet me and it seemed like she could read my mind and meet my needs. That was when I was ten years old. To have those same expectations at age forty-five is a distortion of thirty-five years. I'm no longer ten and Hannah isn't my mother.

There were many years when I didn't admit this was going on. I didn't **re**veal myself. I hid. This caused a lot of confusion in my relating with Hannah. There were times when I'd be angry because I wasn't getting what I wanted and she wouldn't know why I was angry. The worst part of this was I didn't know why either, or I was too embarrassed to acknowledge what was going on.

Tom: How about today?

Jake: Over the past several years—since embracing **Reology**— I've become less judgmental, less self-critical. As a result, I'm a lot more honest with myself and with Hannah. Being honest helps us to sort out what's appropriate and what's not appropriate for us to expect from one another.

Tom: I think you're saying that until you sort out what you call "distorted thinking," your responses to situations may be inappropriate.

Jake: Yes, and until we sort out our distortions it's very hard to really be healthy.

Tom: So, as a psychotherapist, what do you do with people?

16

Jake: Usually when people come to me their lives are out of balance, often because there is some distorted thinking going on. This happens when people see themselves and their lives through outdated ideas and beliefs. As a result their lives are incongruous. I help people **re**discover and **re**define themselves so they become congruent—become who they are best suited to be. Sometimes this requires pushing them further off balance than they already are.

Tom: Why push people off balance if they're already off balance?

Jake: Pushing a person off balance is a way of demonstrating my faith in their ability to **re**gain their balance. We may not even recognize how out of balance we are, because being out of balance becomes so familiar—habitual. The right push can help us wake up, **re**member, and **re**connect with ourselves. And it's not something I do casually. First, I create a safe context. The safety fosters honesty and trust. Once there's trust, I encourage people to work at a very deep level. Much of my work has to do with existential issues such as learning to individuate, coming to understand your own Identity, finding what makes life meaningful to you, understanding how to cope with uncertainty, and coming to terms with death and dying.

Tom: If you can do that in two sessions, I'll sign up.

Jake: I wish I could. Actually, you're a lot like most of the people I work with. My clients are mostly high-functioning adults. I'm not suggesting I do therapy with you, but the issues I work on with people are probably relevant to you.

Tom: Give me some examples of what you mean when you say healthy people respond appropriately.

Jake: Responding appropriately means that I respond to what's going on now. I live in the present. If something sad happens, I feel sad. Maybe I cry and I fully experience my sadness. When it's appropriate, I move on. If something disappointing happens in my life, I experience my disappointment, do whatever is appropriate to the circumstances and move on. I can be aggressive when I need to be aggressive, or soft and vulnerable when that's what is called for. I can withhold or be generous, whichever is appropriate.

If I'm healthy I don't resist what's going on in my life right now, today. I don't hold onto outdated ways of being. Bringing the past into the present distorts the present. For example, I don't deny my aging process and make myself unhappy because I'm physically unable to do the things I did when I was twenty years younger. I don't stay in a dysfunctional relationship just because once upon a time my partner was good to me. To stay —if the relationship is no longer healthy—would be to distort reality.

If I'm healthy, I don't limit myself based on some early childhood criticisms from my parents. Instead, I go out in the world and get some current-day feedback to help me understand what I'm capable of doing. I don't withhold from relationships because of my fear of abandonment that stems from having been abandoned earlier in my life. Instead, I **re**veal my fears and concerns; I find appropriate ways to protect myself instead of relying on outdated ways to protect myself.

Tom: I'm getting an image of people hiding inside of their distorted thoughts, kind of living with outdated ideas, and you want them to come out of hiding.

Jake: Yes, because we're not likely to find our health when we're hiding. When we're hiding we're only living partial lives. We're not fully here. That makes it hard to respond appropriately.

Tom: It's not always so easy to come out of hiding. I've tried. I've even tried some therapy. Sometimes it helped, other times it didn't. You remember that line in a Rod Stewart song, "Some times you have to fake it until you make it." I think sometimes that's all we can do.

Jake: Sure, I remember. That's how I lived in my teens and early twenties. And I agree with you that it's not always easy to come out of hiding but then, once we do, life is easier because we're free to be ourselves. As for therapy, different forms of therapy work for different people. My approach to therapy is based on **Re**ology.

Tom: Which is something you created?

Jake: Hannah and I, yes, and together we're standing on other people's shoulders.

Tom: And how is this different from other psychological models?

Jake: Most significantly, **Re**ology teaches us a new way to use language. Language is the primary way that we make meaning. If we change the way we use language, we change the meaning of our lives.

The way we talk to ourselves and other people determines the quality of our relationships. And so we've adapted what we learned from our mentors to create **Re**Speak.

The brilliance of **Re**Speak is the emphasis that we place on the prefix RE. These two letters **re**veal the possibility we have to **re**think every situation, **re**do our behaviors and **re**turn to now.

Tom: How is that possible?

Jake: Because what's happening every moment is that our brains are creating **re**presentations of the world we're observing. I want to repeat what I just said, we create **re**presentations of the world—we **re**-present the world to ourselves—moment by moment. The two letters RE are used to mean that we do something again. What we're doing, again and again, is **re**creating the world "out there" within ourselves. And because this is a continuous process, we can intervene at any moment and make choices—choices to behave differently, choices to be more conscious, choices to open up instead of shut down.

We've found that after people learn **Re**Speak, almost every time they use a RE word—and there are over four thousand of them—these words serve as little reminders that we have a choice in how we **re**spond to people and to the world.

Tom: So all the RE words are like little alarm clocks.

Jake: Exactly! When we use **Re**Speak we wake ourselves up. Every time we speak is a chance to elevate our consciousness.

Tom: This sounds incredibly liberating.

Jake: Yes, for me, there's a really interesting combination of liberating myself while simultaneously choosing to be more responsible. I liberate myself because any time I make a mistake, or behave in ways I **re**gret, I can **re**do myself.

At the same time I feel more responsible because I **re**cognize that I have choices. One of my favorite quotes comes from Aldous Huxley, who said that experience is not what happens to you; it's what you do with what happens to you.

So, yes, **Re**ology celebrates our potential to live fully, to liberate ourselves, and to pursue happiness, but while asking us to take greater personal **re**sponsibility. The word "responsibility" is based on the word "response." We're responsible for however we respond to what happens to us.

Tom: What you're saying is that this isn't just a "feel good" philosophy.

Jake: No, **Re**ology's more than that. **Re**ology asks us to face up to the challenges that are unique to our time. We live in a world of limited resources. We not only have limited natural resources, but we limit our human resources.

We limit ourselves by fearing people who are different from us. We limit ourselves by tolerating our own immaturity. We limit ourselves by fighting to be right. We limit ourselves by denying our impermanence. These limitations put our planet at peril, make casualties out of our children, and prevent us from fulfilling our human potential.

And just like switching from fossil fuel to alternative fuels is a radical change, **Re**ology involves a radical **re**orientation in the way we think about life and ourselves and other people.

CHAPTER 2

Who Is The Architect of Your Life?

When I was nineteen, I bought three acres of wooded land in Vermont. I planned to build a log cabin, but I knew nothing about construction. Tom had spent some time as a carpenter and offered to help me. We lived together and worked side by side through a long, snowy winter. It was a crazy time of year to build a house in Vermont, but we persevered, and by the end of summer we had created a beautiful three-story log home.

During that time, Tom grew a beard and turned into a lumberjack. I think it was one of his happiest times. He talked about becoming an architect—which I think he would have loved —but it was a dream he never pursued.

Tom: Why do you refer to **Re**ology as radical?

Jake: Because it eliminates even the subtlest forms of violence. That's radical.

Tom: Which leads to what?

Jake: No violence. No victims.

Tom: That would go a long way to eliminate suffering. A very Buddhist concept, isn't it?

Jake: Absolutely. Buddhism is committed to eliminating suffering for all sentient beings and so is **Re**ology.

Tom: What do you do in your spare time?

Jake: I'm serious; I believe this work is the basis for solving our most serious problems. It realistically provides a means for us to peacefully coexist.

Tom: So what's in the secret sauce?

Jake: There are many ingredients. The most crucial one is understanding that each of us assigns meaning to everything that happens in our lives and then we call it "reality," but what we call reality is not necessarily an accurate reflection of what's going on "out there." It's a reflection of what's going on "in us."

If we truly understand this, then the source of control—and responsibility—in our lives shifts from being external to being internal. This radically alters our relationship to everything and everyone. If we really step into this paradigm we'll turn our lives upside down and inside out and challenge our fundamental ideas about reality.

Tom: Which is a good thing?

Jake: A great thing. We become the architects of our own lives. We determine who we are and what's meaningful to us. We stop acting as if other people are doing things to us, which means we stop being reactive or behaving like a child. Instead, we become proactive and behave like responsible adults.

Tom: I'm listening.

Jake: The idea is very simple. I'm not responding to the world, I'm responding to the way I make meaning of the world.

We go through our lives and experience all sorts of stimuli that come from external sources. We receive the stimuli through our sensory systems in the forms of sound, sight, smell, taste, and touch. Those are the standard five senses we usually refer to. But there are several other ways through which we experience the stimuli in our lives. These include our ability to sense hot and cold, light pressure and deep pressure, pain, balance, body movement, tickling, and geomagnetic orientation. Some of us are uniquely sensitive to certain forms of stimulation while being unaware of or insensitive to others. Each of us experiences these external stimuli in a unique way.

We each have individual filters that further modify our experiences of the stimuli. Our filters are made up of a combination of our genetics, memories, education, ethnic and cultural background, age stages, gender, values, cognitive and physical capabilities, as well as traumatic events, and all the other factors that make us unique.

All incoming stimuli are edited and altered by these filters and this process creates our individual consciousness. My individual, conditioned consciousness becomes my projection of reality. It's the way that I make meaning of the incoming stimulus. I'll make meaning, or create my consciousness, in a way that is entirely unique to me. I'll make meaning of events to reinforce my ideas about the world and my Identity. I'll then respond to what's in my consciousness with thoughts, feelings, and actions. So, I'm not responding to the world, I'm responding to the way I make meaning of the world.

Tom: This is making me think of the scientist John Wheeler, who said, "There is no out there out there—we are all observers in the universe—it's a miracle that we construct the same vision of it." I think Wheeler was coming at this from a slightly different angle, but my sense is that he was talking about something very similar to what I hear you saying.

Jake: Yes, very similar. But I'm saying we actually don't construct the same vision of the universe. Because we each have our own set of filters, by the time any stimulus travels through our filters, even if it was the same stimulus, the end result will be different. This means that I'm making up my meaning of the world in my own way, and you're doing so in your own way. When I tell you about my experiences, I'm not telling you about the world "out there," I'm telling you about my world "in me."

There's a Zen poem that says, "To her lover, a beautiful woman is a delight; to an ascetic, a distraction; to a wolf, a good meal."

Tom: Then two people are never talking about exactly the same thing.

Jake: I'm talking about what's in my consciousness and you're talking about what's in your consciousness.

Tom: Does this mean that a shared experience is an illusion?

Jake: It means illusions are shared experiences. Or, as another Buddhist author wrote, "We're not denying the ordinary perception we have of the world. What we are denying is that, in the final analysis, the world has any intrinsic reality."

Tom: But practically speaking what do you do with this?

Jake: If we accept that there is no intrinsic reality, we become curious about the different ways people see the world. We stop telling people the way the world is or how they should be. We don't act as if we know what's best for another person, because we can't truly know that person; we can only know our idea of them. With this shift in perspective people become less defensive, less guarded.

Tom: If some guy comes up to you and tells you that you're a jerk, you don't feel defensive?

Jake: I might be taken aback if it's a surprise to me. If the guy looks angry, my adrenaline might kick in so I can fight or run away. But quickly, very quickly—as soon as I know I'm not in physical danger—I become curious. I wonder, why does he perceive me as a jerk? What idea is he holding of me? Who am I to him? I'm curious about it all.

26

Tom: So you never get defensive?

Jake: Sure, I still get defensive, but I've become much less defensive since I started seeing the world in this way.

Tom: I'm not inclined to argue with what you're saying. It seems rather obvious to me that we're only talking about our own perceptions of the world.

Jake: Yet, we speak as if we're talking about one objective world "out there," not our perceptions of the world. We spend a great deal of time telling people the way it is, the way they are, the way they should be. We fight about who said what and who meant what. Often, even people who understand this concept speak in a way that's incongruent with their intentions because ordinary language tends to objectify what we talk about. So even when we don't mean to tell people the way the world is, we often do just that—we talk as if there's one objective reality.

Tom: So, instead of telling other people the way things are—objectively—you want me to see the world through their eyes, even when I may strongly disagree with them. You're suggesting that everything is relative, but there are some things in life that are right and others that are wrong.

Jake: Actually, I'm saying that you can't see the world through the eyes of others, only your eyes. We each see the world through our own eyes and we justify what we see so the world makes sense to us. Think about that! Then, most of us act as if what we see is the truth, but it's not.

And yes, I believe the meaning we make is relative. We establish the meaning of one thing in relationship to other things.

Tom: Isn't anything absolute in your mind?

Jake: Many things are absolute, but they only become absolute after I've established some hierarchy of values. I think the sanctity of human life is absolute, but that's a value I've accepted. It's absolute for me, but not everyone may agree. I recognize that relativism is a slippery slope, because it can result in people never taking a stand. The notion of "live and let live" gets complicated when we live in an interconnected world.

Tom: It gets complicated just within a family.

Jake: True enough.

Tom: So what's your solution?

Jake: **Re**ology is a solution because it illuminates the subjective nature of our experiences. It then teaches us a new way to communicate—one that conveys this subjectivity, which fosters greater understanding and empathy.

Tom: My sense is that some people have empathy and other people don't. I don't think empathy is easy to teach.

Jake: There's an excellent book, *The First Idea*, which explores empathy. The authors say that empathy grows whenever we cultivate certain characteristics in our lives. It grows when we feel personally secure because then we're more open to points of view that differ from our own. It grows as we become comfortable with a broad range of emotions because this increases our capacity to understand and connect with other people. It grows when we live our lives according to our own values because then we stop measuring ourselves based upon other people's values. It grows when we learn how to have conversations in which we talk about our perceptions instead of speaking as if we're talking about facts and using those facts to make people wrong.

Reology cultivates all of these characteristics: personal security, comfort with a broader range of emotions, living according to our own mature values, and learning to have perception-oriented conversation in which no one is made wrong.

Tom: If you want to cultivate empathy I think you should be working with kids. Start when they're young.

Jake: That definitely makes it easier, but I think we have to start wherever we find ourselves. This is so important to the future of our species. We live with other people—partners, kids, communities, countries—and we must find respectful ways to address our differences.

I'm convinced that the key to doing this is to alter the way we use language because language underlies the whole way in which we make meaning and think about the world.

A minute ago you said it seems obvious to you that we are only talking about our perceptions of the world. I said that's not actually how we talk, but it is possible to talk that way. This gets us to the actual practice of **Re**ology that I want to share with you, which includes learning **Re**Speak—a new way to communicate, a new language structure that shows us how to **re**create our lives.

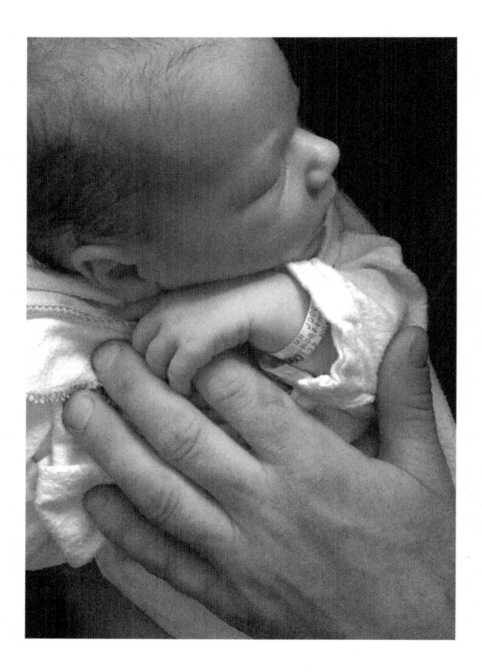

CHAPTER 3

Stewards of a Legacy:
John and Joyce Weir

We took a break to have a cup of tea. I had tea, and as usual, Tom had water. For over twenty years he hadn't had tea, coffee, sugar, or anything else he thought was bad for him. He was a health fanatic, often exercising as much as three hours a day. I believe he thought this was his way of ensuring a long and healthy life.

Tom: You created your own new language?

Jake: It's not exactly a new language, but rather a new structure that can be applied to many languages. We teach this to people who speak English as well as German, Japanese and Spanish. And we didn't create this way of speaking, we're stewards of this language; it was created by John and Joyce Weir. Do you remember that for several years Hannah and I studied with an elderly couple?

Tom: Vaguely.

Jake: Well, John Weir was a psychologist, and along with his wife Joyce, they developed a unique philosophy—really, it's a way of living. They called it Percept. One thing that makes Percept so significant is that it includes a new way to use language.

Tom: Percept comes from the word perception?

Jake: Yes. At the core of Percept is the understanding that we each create our own distinct perception of everything in our lives.

John and Joyce had about ten thousand people attend their workshops, people from all walks of life. Corporations sent their leaders. Married couples came to improve their relationships. Individuals came who were searching for happiness. John and Joyce were pioneers in the human potential movement. They both retired at the age of eighty-five, and Hannah and I are carrying on their work. John died in 2006.

Tom: When did you meet them?

Jake: I think it was 1999. John and I felt a special connection with one another from the moment we met. We had very different backgrounds, but we arrived at similar conclusions about human nature and how to work with people. John had a doctorate in clinical psychology and had been on the faculty at the University of California. My experience came from running companies, studying group dynamics, and being in private practice. John and I shared many of the same ideas about how to facilitate personal growth and how to do psychotherapy. We both believed in being very candid with clients, personally revealing, and using our relationship with our clients as our primary therapeutic tool. We both focused on structure and didn't get overly absorbed in our client's content.

Tom: I don't know what you mean.

Jake: *What* people talk about is the content. *How* they talk about it is the structure. Regardless of what you talk about, do you talk about it as a self-empowered man or do you talk about it as a victim? Do you talk about the world impacting you, or about how you impact the world? Do you talk about the past and future, or do you talk and live in the present moment? Do you hold an optimistic perspective or a pessimistic perspective? These are just a few examples of structure. As a therapist, you have much more leverage to help someone grow when you work at a structural level. John and I shared a passion about this; it's why we were both fascinated with language because to a therapist, language can be what a sword is to a samurai.

Tom: And John was your sensei?

Jake: He was. Hannah and I went to the last training that John and Joyce put on before they retired. After their final training we spent as much time as we could with them. They visited our home and we would fly out to California to spend time together. We did this for about six years and during that time we started conducting our own trainings and received mentoring from John and Joyce.

Hannah and Joyce seemed to connect as well as John and I did. Joyce was in charge of the physical part of their trainings, which included movement, dance, and all sorts of fascinating ways of ensuring the mind and body were integrated during the training. She led their students through experiential activities that were intentionally designed to help people more fully experience themselves. Both of us were lucky to have such mentors.

For us, John and Joyce have been remarkable examples of people who were healthy in every way. I love the fact that they were still teaching in their mid-eighties, taking their work on the road and driving across the country in an old Winnebago, teaching one workshop after another. Their trainings were life-changing events for many people. I hope Hannah and I are still teaching these workshops when we're in our eighties.

One of the great things about the Weirs was that they were an example of what they taught. John developed a model showing the ten stages of development that humans may grow through. He and Joyce were examples of people who had grown through all ten stages.

Tom: You say people "may" grow through these stages?

Jake: It's up to each of us. Not everyone keeps growing.

Tom: Good point.

Jake: And John and Joyce were examples of people who kept choosing to grow—they stepped fully into themselves and were unique, interesting, and enlivening to be around. They were also incredibly healthy, sharp, and vibrant.

Tom: What made them so healthy?

Jake: I asked John that question because a lot of people were impressed with the way he and Joyce aged so gracefully. John said he couldn't speak for Joyce, but that his health was the result of being so relaxed. He told me a story about how when he was a young man he needed to wear glasses. Then he married Joyce, whose mother was a Bates vision instructor. She taught him a different way to use his eyes that was based on learning to relax his vision. He learned to see by relaxing, not by straining to see, and he believed that was a metaphor for how we can live in the world. When John told me this story he was ninety and he still didn't need glasses.

In my experience, a large part of his health had to do with his lack of resistance to living, to aging, and to dying. John didn't waste any of his energy resisting things. Both he and Joyce were unusually present to whatever was happening in the moment. They were both wide awake and original in the way they thought about things and the way they lived their lives. They wrote, directed, and starred in their own life stories. They didn't fit into any conceptual straitjackets.

For over thirty years they taught at National Training Laboratories in Bethel, Maine. NTL was, and probably still is, on the cutting edge of the human potential movement. When Joyce and John were teaching there, it was a time of great excitement in the field of human potential.

One of the big things during that time was for group members to practice giving direct feedback to other group members. Along came John saying, "You can't give people feedback because you're not telling people about them, you're always telling them about you." This was a radical idea then and it still is today.

Tom: I'm surprised that ten thousand people have been through their trainings and learned about Percept, yet I've never heard of it.

Jake: Well, the people who learn Percept don't proselytize. They don't tell other people how they should live or what they should do. And John thought it was very difficult to convey Percept through the written word. He never wrote much about it. He believed it's best learned through direct experience.

Tom: If John thought it was so hard to convey, why are you trying to write about it?

Jake: Because my passion is to make this accessible to more people. The best way to learn this is experientially—while attending a retreat—but only a limited number of people will be able to take advantage of that opportunity. When people read about this they won't get it to the same degree they would by immersing themselves in one of our retreats, but I believe they'll still benefit. And I want that to happen because I haven't experienced a more powerful self-improvement model.

After learning Percept my life significantly changed for the better. I had been consciously working on myself for over twenty-five years, trying all sorts of things, but nothing had the impact of Percept. Relating with Hannah became so easy. I discovered a way of viewing the world that allows me to make sense of just about everything I see or experience. I find this incredibly comforting and exciting. I believe that if enough people adopt this way of living, we can create a more peaceful and compassionate world.

Hannah and I have made this our life's work. We've taken the body of work that John and Joyce developed, and we've allowed it to evolve into **Re**ology, which is easier to learn and use in your life. I think we've made it more digestible and sticky. And we hope this will attract more people.

We continue John and Joyce's tradition of emphasizing this truly unique way of using language. There are many ways in which **Re**ology distinguishes itself from other psychological models and communication skills, but the one that stands out the most for me is that **Re**Speak completely alters the level of conversations we have—with ourselves and other people.

CHAPTER 4

The Language of Renewal: *ReSpeak*

One of my favorite memories of being with Tom was when the two of us were lying on our parents' bed watching television. It's strange how vivid this memory is for me. We were on our stomachs with our heads at the foot of the bed. The television was only about four feet in front of our faces.

The position we were in was pretty uncomfortable, so during the commercial breaks we would turn our heads sideways and look at each other. I don't know why, maybe it was because of how physically close we were to one another, but each of us thought the other looked ridiculous. We would look at each other and just start laughing. It was kind of like looking in those mirrors they have in fun houses, the ones that make you look goofy.

We weren't little kids in this memory; I guess we were probably in our early twenties. This is one of very few memories I have of us belly-laughing together.

Tom: Tell me about the mechanics of the language. How do you use it and what does it do?

Jake: The language that John and Joyce called Percept, we now refer to as **ReSpeak**, and when I use it several things happen. I empower myself. I create a sense of motion in my life. I live in the present moment. I increase my self-awareness. I become more relaxed, creative, and less anxious.

Tom: I understand being relaxed and living in the moment, but what exactly does it mean to be empowered and create a sense of motion in your life?

Jake: To me, being empowered is the opposite of feeling like a victim. When I empower myself I know that I'm creating the meaning of all my experiences. I don't feel as if people are doing things to me. And when I say I create a sense of motion in my life, what I mean is that I don't feel stuck—emotionally stuck or stuck in old patterns of behavior. Using **Re**Speak helps me recognize that everything is temporary and malleable.

Tom: And you also said ReSpeak reduces your anxiety, but I'm unclear how language relates to anxiety.

Jake: The way we use language—the way we talk to ourselves— turns the volume up and down in different parts of the brain. Anxiety is often the result of triggering parts of the brain that should be left quiet—left to protect us in the case of a real threat. **Re**Speak helps us use our brains by encouraging each part to do what it does best. When we learn how to do this, we reduce our anxiety.

Tom: That's a lot to promise.

Jake: It's a lot to promise, but this isn't pie-in-the-sky. It's a very practical approach to empowering one's self, to get unstuck, to live in the present, to be more self-aware, and to reduce anxiety.

Tom: If all that really happens, I'll send Vicky and the kids to your next training.

Jake: What about you?

Tom: We'll see.

Jake: I'd love to have you come to one of our trainings.

Tom: This is my training. What's step number one?

Jake: There are two overarching rules and two guidelines.

Rule # 1: **Re**Turn To Now

Return to now means we speak about what's happening in the present moment. We waste so much time when we argue about who said what when. What really matters is *now*—that's where the action is—everything is happening now.

Tom: What if I'm upset about something you did last week?

Jake: Are you upsetting yourself now, in this moment?

Tom: Yes.

Jake: Then, **return to now** and let's talk about what's going on for you right now. Let's not get lost in who did what last week, or who said what…because we probably won't agree. We probably remember things differently, and we can't change the past. We only have now.

Tom: I like it. It seems very direct and mature.

Jake: That's why I refer to this way of speaking as having adult/adult conversations. Okay…

Rule # 2: **Re**Move Praise and Blame

We want to **re**move praise and blame because both praise and blame are short-term ways of controlling people that have negative long-term consequences. They're both based on the dualistic distinctions of "good" and "bad." Such judgments turn "on" the fear centers in our brains and lead to dependency and defensiveness.

Dependency occurs when I seek praise from another person, using it as a way to feel good about myself. Defensiveness occurs because I fear other people's judgment that comes in the form of blame. By **re**moving praise, I'm less likely to seek my sense of self from others. By **re**moving blame, I stop fearing being judged, so I'm more willing to **re**veal myself, which always results in clarity, and sometimes results in greater intimacy.

Tom: That's stupid.

Jake: Clearly you've got the hang of **re**moving blame.

Tom: No, I'm just kidding. I get the idea, although I think it's totally unrealistic, but keep going.

Jake: I just want you to consider how freeing it could be to step out of the praise/blame, right/wrong way of communicating. What if we could eliminate our fear of other people's judgments? What if we stopped looking to other people to determine our okay-ness?

Tom: I'm not disputing that it would be valuable, just that it seems unrealistic.

Jake: I want to talk more about this later, but for now just try to keep an open mind. I want to introduce you to the guidelines so you have the complete picture.

Tom: What's the difference between rules and guidelines?

Jake: The rules are always applicable. The guidelines are more specific and they vary depending on what you're talking about. But they all have one thing in common, which is speaking as if you are responsible for yourself.

Guideline # 1: **Re**Source Your Feelings

The way we do this with **Re**Speak is to ask ourselves one simple question: "What am I doing to myself?"

Tom: What's the point of the question?

Jake: When I use common language to express myself, if I'm feeling frustrated or angry, I'll say things like, "This is frustrating," or "You make me angry." But when I use **Re**Speak, and I answer the question, "What am I doing to myself?" my response is different. I'll say, "I frustrate myself," or "I anger myself." I am *resourcing my feelings*. The source of my feelings isn't *out there*; my feelings originate within me.

I own my feelings and inner experiences when I use language in this way. I empower myself. No one is doing these things to me. You aren't frustrating me or making me angry. I'm doing this to myself. And if I do X to myself, maybe I can stop and do Y. If I feel frustrated, that's because I frustrate myself. If I feel angry, you're not making me angry; I do this to myself. When I use **Re**Speak I take responsibility for what I do to myself.

Tom: If you call me a liar, I'm going to get upset and you're the cause of me getting upset. I don't see how I'm doing that to myself.

Jake: Well, you have a choice. You can give me the power to determine how you feel, in which case it's as if I'm running your nervous system, or you can realize that we simply see things in different ways. And you can be curious about our differences.

So, if *you* call *me* a liar, my response is going to be to ask you why you think that. Maybe you heard something other than what I intended you to hear, maybe we just have a misunderstanding—I don't know—but I'm choosing to be curious instead of reactive.

Tom: I don't think most people could do that, respond that way.

Jake: We can if we take the time to learn **Re**Speak. And there is a great precedent for speaking this way. The language that the Buddha spoke, Pali, was a "verbing" language. It allowed one to stay in process, not fixing oneself or clinging to a static or permanent state, but expressing oneself as being in motion— unfolding—which is a foundational premise of Buddhism. For example, in Pali, "Nirvana," would not be a noun but a verb— Nirvana-ing ourselves—actively putting out fires of greed, hatred and delusion. Instead of "enlightenment" being a static state that we try to achieve, the Buddha recommended "enlighten-ing" ourselves— an active, continuous process. **Re**Speak is a modern-day equivalent to this perspective and way of speaking.

Tom: That's fascinating. So when you're talking about your feelings you put the feeling after the word "I." "I excite myself," "I disappoint myself." You turn the feeling into a verb.

Jake: Exactly. The feeling occurs in me, so I own the feeling—I am taking ownership of myself. And there are a few ways we can "verb" ourselves.

"I <u>am delighting</u> myself."

"I <u>frustrate</u> myself."

"I <u>make myself</u> sad."

Tom: Which do you use when?

Jake: Play around with them. Notice how you feel. There is no right way or wrong way. The different ways offer you some flexibility. I'd rather say, "I make myself sad," instead of saying, "I sad myself." That's because "sad" is an adjective and usually adjectives will sound more natural when you use "make" as the verb: "I make myself _____."

44

One more thing. If you're describing your feelings or inner experience, change "it" to "I" at the beginning of a sentence, or change "it" to "myself" at the end of a sentence. For example, there's no "it" that disappoints me. Instead of saying, "It was disappointing," I say, "I disappoint myself." Instead of saying, "I feel good about it," I say, "I feel good about myself." The same with other pronouns, there's no "she" who makes me feel bad. There may be a "she" who does something, but I'm the one who makes meaning of what "she" has done. And from that meaning I make myself feel the way I do. So instead of saying, "She makes me angry," I say, "I anger myself" or "I make myself angry."

In any of these examples if you need to tack on more information, you just add "with" or "when" and fill in the details. "I disappoint myself *when* you don't call to tell me you'll be late."

Tom: This makes a lot of sense to me, especially given that we're talking about things that are going on internally. But what happens when I talk about an event that I observe?

Jake: That brings us to the next guideline.

Guideline # 2: **Re**Spect Our Differences

When I'm talking about something other than a feeling—like an event—I use **Re**Speak to be clear that I'm talking about my perception of the event, not the event itself. The same is true if I talk about a belief I have. There is a very simple structure we use to do this. For example, instead of saying, "Always being honest is the best thing," I would say:

"I perceive <u>always being honest</u> as <u>the best thing</u>."

Tom: So you're always talking about your perception or interpretation, instead of being emphatic about the way things are.

Jake: Yes, when talking about anything other than a feeling, I make it clear that I'm only talking about my interpretation, my perception, or my understanding of the event or idea. I own my perception and don't need to argue about who's right or wrong because I'm aware that we all have our own unique way of making meaning of what we observe.

Years ago Hannah and I were driving near Boulder, Colorado. We saw a meteor streak across the sky and smash into a hillside just a couple of miles away. Hannah started talking about the meteor with great excitement, describing it as bright green. I interrupted her and said, "Green? It was white." She used **Re**Speak and said, "I perceived it as green." She didn't say, "It was green."

This may seem like a subtle distinction, but using **Re**Speak has eliminated the majority of our petty disagreements and unnecessary arguing. Prior to learning this way of speaking, we would have had an argument, each trying to make the other person wrong. Instead, we created a space for curiosity. We were amazed that we could perceive the same object so differently.

With **Re**Speak, we're aware that everything we observe is seen through our personal filters. By the time any event comes through these filters, it's no longer external; it has become my perception. If I'm aware of this, I can own my perception and know that others have their own perceptions, and this allows me to **re**spect our differences. The simplest way to express myself is to say: "I perceive the meteor as green."

Tom: Why not just say, "The meteor looks green to me."

Jake: That's fine. It's just that most of the time we don't say, "This is how X looks to me." We say, "This is what X is." We act as though what we see is factual. We try to objectify things. But we can't convey an objective reflection of the world; we can only convey how we see the world.

If we use expressions such as "I perceive X as _____," we're making clear to ourselves and to others that we're only talking about our way of making meaning of some event. And when I go out in the world and use an expression such as, "I perceive this as a beautiful day," most people have no problem understanding what I'm saying.

Tom: It seems a tad awkward to me.

Jake: Well, you can use other expressions that may sound less awkward. "I see X as _____." "I experience X as _____." "I interpret X as _____." Also, part of the value in learning **Re**Speak, or doing anything new, is that we stop running on autopilot. We become more intentional.

Tom: Okay, let me test-drive this language. When I'm frustrated, I could say, "I frustrate myself." When I feel angry I can say, "I make myself angry." When I talk about an event or an idea, I might say, "I experience life as difficult," or "I perceive global warming as a serious problem." This is what I'm doing. Someone else might talk about these same things in a completely different way.

Jake: Exactly.

Tom: So using this language, how do I talk about other people?

Jake: You either talk about what you're doing to yourself with them, for example, "*I nurture myself* having this conversation with you," or, you talk about your perceptions of them. For example I might say, "I perceive you as curious." This is quite different from telling you, "You are curious." And there are times, using **Re**Speak, when we make a distinction between you —sitting over there—and you in my mind, but this is more nuanced and something that we teach only in our retreats.

Tom: To me it sounds like what you're doing is making very explicit distinctions about what's factual and what is a subjective perception.

Jake: Yes, and as we continue exploring this, you may notice that I think most of what we talk about is subjective, especially when it comes to relationships. Do you feel the difference?

Tom: I do. As I listen to you talk, I'm finding this easier to grasp. No matter what you tell me about, you're telling me about your experience and your perception. Everything "out there," by the time it travels through your filters, becomes a part of you, your version of what's out there.

Jake: Yes. This really isn't complicated. However, using **Re**Speak is a radically different way of experiencing and expressing ourselves.

Tom: I'm beginning to get a sense of that. But I'd like you to give me another example. Let's imagine that you think I've been disrespectful towards you. How would you address me using ReSpeak, without telling me about me?

Jake: I would say, "Tom, I disrespect myself with what you said." This is what I do to myself. You may have told me a joke you thought was funny, but I didn't think the joke was funny at all—I disrespect myself with the joke. This is what I am doing within myself.

Tom: I love the simplicity of that.

Jake: Using **Re**Speak you could say, "I simplify myself with this language."

Tom: This is fascinating…I fascinate myself. And if I boil all of this down, I really only have to verb myself: "I frustrate myself," "I delight myself," and when talking about events or beliefs I start sentences by saying, "I perceive X as _____."

Jake: I think that's basically true. You can start learning **Re**Speak just by "verbing" yourself and using expressions such as, "I perceive X as _____." That's a really good start. The other suggestion I have is *return to now*—speak about what's happening right now—and *remove praise and blame*.

Tom: Do you have any other suggestions to help me learn ReSpeak?

Jake: Hand me that napkin and I'll write down my crib sheet version:

2 RULES OF RESPEAK

ReTurn to Now

ReMove Praise and Blame

2 GUIDELINES OF RESPEAK

ReSource Your Feelings

ReSpect Our Differences

I've found that the best way to learn **Re**Speak is to slow down, pay exquisite attention to your internal experience, and describe how you are making sense to yourself. Answer the question, "What am I doing to or within myself?"

Tom: To express myself using ReSpeak, I guess I'd say that I tire myself. It's not that I'm not interested, but I'm going to nap for a while, then the next time we talk we can pick up where we're leaving off.

Between this conversation and the next, his world and my world changed and would never be the same.

Tom's headaches got worse; he started losing his balance and was unable to deny that something was seriously wrong. Visits with various doctors confirmed that he had an inoperable brain tumor.

After learning of his illness, Tom and I spoke by phone. He seemed strangely detached. I kept repeating that I just couldn't believe what he was telling me. It didn't make sense; how could he be so sick?

Jake: Two months ago you were running three miles a day.

Tom: Five miles.

Jake: Okay, five. That's my point. How can you be so healthy and so sick?

Tom: I don't know, but we've had three doctors confirm the same thing.

Jake: So what will you do? What can I do? This is so terrible.

Tom: Jake, I don't think there's really anything you can do. I'll go through the treatments they recommend, but my sense is this is just about buying some time.

Jake: How are you dealing with this? Do you have helpful people you can talk with, maybe a therapist or some kind of support group?

Tom: After the conversation we've been having, it's obvious you know that people deal with things in their own way. I'm not you. I'm not necessarily looking to talk about my feelings. I deal with things in my way.

Jake: Fair enough. You're absolutely right. I guess I just feel helpless so I'm throwing out suggestions.

Tom: I know. I appreciate it but I'll find my own way through this. They say the treatments I need will really zap me, so I'll be spending a lot of time horizontal, which means we can continue our conversation.

Jake: You're dealing with a life-threatening illness and you want to continue our conversation? I'm flattered, but we don't need to do that. Let's wait and see how you feel.

Tom: Don't be flattered, think of yourself as entertainment. I need to distract myself. I'd like to continue our conversation. I also think that some of your ideas are helpful to me. Maybe this is my way of dealing with things. Instead of talking about my feelings I can sort them out as we continue talking.

Jake: Are you sure?

Tom: Respect my wishes. I have my reasons. Maybe I'll share more about them with you later. For now, let's just keep going....

So after a brief pause we continued. At first I wondered, was I enabling Tom's denial? But the more we talked, the more I came to believe that talking about theories and ideas was a comfortable way for Tom to explore the new territory in which he found himself. As he said, we each deal with things in our own ways. I also believed that even if our conversation was about ideas, and not a direct expression of our feelings, we were connecting in a more intimate way than we ever had before.

CHAPTER 5

Remove Praise and Blame

After finding out about Tom's illness, I felt terribly awkward in my life. If I started to fully relax or have a good time, I felt as though I shouldn't be doing so. Every time the phone rang, I startled myself, afraid it was bad news. Everything I read seemed dull or trivial.

The only time I felt reasonably good was when I was working. I was honest with my clients, letting them know about Tom. The depth at which I work with people requires complete honesty; I didn't want to hold back something as significant as Tom's illness or I would have felt like I wasn't honoring the relationship I have with my clients.

Some of them expressed reluctance to talk about their problems because, in comparison, their problems seemed insignificant. In some cases, I reassured clients that their problems were deserving of attention. In other cases, I used my brother's illness to point out to clients that they were wasting energy on trivial matters. I used his illness to create perspective—for them and me.

When my conversation with Tom continued, he shared with me how worried he was about the people closest to him—how they were being affected by his illness. He blamed himself for making their lives more difficult. He talked quite a bit about his daughter, Clarissa. She was in her first year of college and Tom missed her living at home, though he was happy to see her starting her own life. He didn't want his illness to burden her, but feared it did, and he was also concerned about our parents. He wanted them to enjoy life in their eighties. He said that when they were happy, it helped him believe life was fair, because of all the people he knew, they most deserved to be happy.

My brother was a romantic. I liked that about him.

Jake: Do you really want to keep talking about this? It feels weird to me. How are you doing?

Tom: I know you're trying to be helpful but I don't feel like talking about myself right now. Our conversation is a good distraction for me. Let's just keep talking.

The last time we spoke you were suggesting that the best way to learn ReSpeak is to pay attention to my internal experience and describe how I'm making sense to myself. You also said that's a lot easier to do if you remove praise and blame, but this idea of no praise and no blame seems completely unrealistic. For one thing, I'm not sure that praise and blame are always bad and, for another, I know very few people who don't rely on a lot of praise and some blame to control their kids.

Jake: But notice that your example is about kids and you're suggesting that we need to control them.

Tom: At times we do.

Jake: I agree, at times we do. My point is that praise and blame are often used when we want to control other people, but do we want to control adults?

Tom: Before we talk about adults, what about kids?

Jake: As a parent, at first, giving up praise and blame is a lot more work. But, over time, children who aren't controlled with praise and blame become healthier people.

Tom: In what way?

Jake: Blame encourages us to hide. Not a helpful message to send to kids or to anyone. And surprisingly, praise can encourage us to hide, as well. If you express your high opinion of me by praising me, I may hide my "bad parts" to avoid disappointing you. Also, if I rely on your praise to feel good about myself, I've put my nervous system in your hands. If I please you, I feel good. If I don't please you, I feel bad. Children raised without praise and blame learn to look to themselves for validation instead of looking to external sources to find out if they are an okay person. Kids raised in this way seem to have more self-awareness and better self-esteem. They have access to their own internal compass and they rely on themselves for guidance.

Tom: You know kids like that?

Jake: Not a lot, but I've seen a few kids who were raised with this consciousness. They were extremely self-reliant, mature, and comfortable in their own skins.

Tom: Okay, it's too late to change whatever I did with Clarissa and Rand, but your point is to try not to control other people.

Jake: Especially adults. I recognize that sometimes when we deal with kids we need to control them for their own safety, but rarely, if ever, do we need to do this with another adult.

Tom: Maybe we don't need to control them, but we certainly want to be able to praise people as a way to show our appreciation.

Jake: We can express appreciation while using **Re**Speak, but we do so without praise.

Tom: How do you do one without doing the other?

Jake: Praise is me telling you about you. "You're great." "You're terrific!" "You're the best." Appreciation is me telling you about myself or my experience of you. "I appreciate your candor." "I respect the work you do." "I enjoy having this time with you."

Tom: I hear the difference. It makes sense to me, but aren't you concerned that if you assume you aren't telling me anything about me, you'll be more likely to hurt my feelings? I mean you can call me an idiot and then say, "Hey, I'm just talking about my perception of you, I 'm not really talking about you."

Jake: **Re**ology is more than just a way of speaking, it's a philosophy that promotes personal responsibility. And that includes being responsible for the way we treat other people. One of the principles of **Re**ology is "do no harm." **Re**Speak helps us avoid harming people, because we honor and respect the ways in which they are different from us.

Tom: I understand that. Let's go back to the question of blame. I blame myself for not having my life the way I want it. You're suggesting I shouldn't blame myself, but I have a lot of unfinished business, especially if I were to die. That's the way I see it.

Jake: Doesn't blaming yourself just make this harder?

Tom: I suppose so.

Jake: When I feel blamed, and I see this with other people, I tend to become defensive and less resourceful. And what's interesting is that this happens whether I feel blamed by other people or I blame myself.

Tom: Don't you think we can use blame to motivate ourselves?

Jake: Is that what you're doing?

Tom: Not really. I'm just making myself feel bad. Are you blaming me for that?

Jake: Not at all.

Tom: What then?

Jake: I'm witnessing you. That's a significant aspect of **Re**ology.

Tom: Meaning what exactly?

Jake: When I witness you, I'm doing my best to understand whatever is going on for you. I have no agenda. I'm not trying to fix you. I'm not giving feedback. I'm just trying to understand your experience.

Tom: I like that concept. And I agree that blaming myself isn't helpful; it isn't the way to go. I'd like to change it.

Jake: Remember that with **ReSpeak** it often helps if we change "it" to "I" at the beginning of sentences and change "it" to "myself" at the end of sentences. So using **ReSpeak**, what you just said would be, "I'd like to change myself."

Tom: Good, that works—yes, it's different—I'd like to change myself.

Jake: Well, let's talk a little bit about change.

Tom: The older I get, the more I've become convinced that people are who they are. Maybe we can make some adjustments, but I'm not sure radical change is really possible.

Jake: Maybe that depends on what we mean by "radical." If you think of radical change as instant transformation, I'm skeptical about that, too. But if you think of radical change as raising our consciousness—over time, I know that's possible. And I think it's radical because, when we elevate our consciousness we change the way we relate with people and we change our view of the world. This means we can change the world-in-us, and that can lead to changing the world. We create most of our problems as a result of the way we think—as a result of our level of consciousness. **Re**ology elevates our consciousness.

Tom: Listening to you reminds me of an Einstein quote: "We cannot solve our problems with the same thinking we used when we created them."

Jake: Exactly. And the first thing I like to think about in a different way is the entire notion of change. Instead of thinking about change, I like to think about growth.

Tom: Doesn't growth lead to change?

Jake: It does, but change doesn't always lead to growth.

CHAPTER 6

Change Doesn't Always Lead to Growth, but Growth Leads to Change

When I was twelve or thirteen, our parents sent both Tom and me to a summer ski camp in Jackson Hole, Wyoming. I remember being proud of Tom because he was the best skier in the camp. He didn't have much to do with me while we were there—he probably didn't want to be slowed down by his younger brother. When the camp was over, I was going back home, while Tom went to another ski camp in Montana.

He waited with me at the airport until it was time for me to board my plane. When it was time for me to leave, I went to hug Tom, but he put his hand out indicating we should shake hands instead of hug. I remember thinking this was a turning point in our relationship—we were supposed to act like men. I disappointed myself terribly but didn't say anything....

Forty-plus years later, at one point during our conversation, I looked at Tom sitting across from me and asked, "Do you want a hug?" He said, "Why?" I said, "Never mind," and we went back to our conversation.

Jake: **Re**ology focuses on growth more than on change. Growth is about the process; change is about the end result. When we focus on growth, we keep our desired outcomes in mind, but most of our attention stays in the present moment—the moment we can most directly affect. When we focus on change, we often take ourselves away from the present moment. The other problem with focusing on change is that we often think that change means getting rid of what we don't like about ourselves. The intent to discard parts of ourselves creates resistance. This decreases the likelihood of change.

Tom: So you focus on growth, but what exactly does that mean? How do we grow?

Jake: There's a five-step process. The first step is **awareness**. This is the starting place, becoming aware of your thoughts, feelings, and behaviors. In our retreats we encourage people to participate in some unusual activities that are designed to stimulate new awareness. Spend a day blindfolded and you're likely to discover some new parts of yourself. Go barefoot, eat your food with your fingers instead of using utensils, feed your partner a meal or eat in complete silence…all of these are ways to stimulate awareness.

To say nothing about learning a new way to use language. The language practice requires us to slow down and pay attention. And living in a community where no one tells you about you, no one uses praise or blame…all of these are intended to stimulate awareness, to help us wake up to ourselves.

The second step is **acceptance** of our thoughts and feelings. And if we encounter some part of ourselves—say a behavior— that we don't like and we don't want to accept, then we look for the need that's behind that behavior. It may be easier to accept the need behind a particular behavior than to accept the behavior.

Say we become aware that we want to connect with someone, but we pull away because we're afraid of being rejected. If we look at the need behind the behavior of pulling away, we discover our need for self-protection. The point is to accept our need and then look for healthier ways to satisfy our needs.

Tom: I'm aware that I may die, but for me to accept it is beyond me right now. My intention is to fight it, not accept it. I don't want to accept it.

Jake: Okay, I think we're talking about different things. I'm talking about the process of growth, and I think you're talking about not wanting to accept a particular result; you want to change the result.

Tom: Exactly.

Jake: Well, there are some things we can change—such as our own immature behaviors—and then there are other things we can't change. And my point is that if we focus on the process of growth, things will either change or not, but either way our experiences along the way will be healthier. I'm not suggesting that you accept death as imminent, but that you accept the feelings and thoughts you have related to whatever's going on for you. This is easier to do if you **re**move praise and blame.

Tom: I'm not ready to accept that I can't change what's happening to me.

Jake: What about accepting your feelings, which sound to me like feelings of defiance.

Tom: Defiance—yes. I'm pissed because I'm probably the healthiest person I know, at least physically. I exercise two hours a day; I haven't eaten sugar or anything bad for me for the last twenty years. I don't smoke or do drugs. I've had incredibly sophisticated health exams that show my body is like that of a twenty-five-year-old. Yeah, I'm pissed.

Jake: I'd piss myself off too.

Tom: Being defiant and pissed isn't helping. So what do I do about it, based on your model?

Jake: You accept how you feel about having such a serious diagnosis. Have you done that?

Tom: It varies. I spend a lot of time trying not to feel what I'm feeling.

Jake: Over the next few days, why don't you see what happens if you accept your feelings? Then the third step is **asking**, "How do I want to do myself?" Other ways to ask this might be: "How do I want to feel?" "How do I want to behave?" "How do I want to use my personal energy?"

I'm suggesting that if you *accept* how you feel, and *ask* this crucial question about how you would like to conduct yourself, something will shift.

Tom: Then what do I do?

Jake: For this process to be effective, you can't just rush through these steps. Even if you do, the fourth step slows things right down. The fourth step is to wait. I often refer to it as **awaiting** because I built this model based on five A's. Here, I'll write them down for you:

THE 5 STEPS OF GROWTH

Awareness

Acceptance

Asking

Awaiting

Acting

The **awaiting** step is a time to assimilate whatever new awareness you've had—to notice the difference between how you do yourself and how you would like to do yourself. It's a time to integrate. It's also a time to rest, to be receptive and patient.

For those of us who tend to be impulsive, this is a valuable step. And for those of us who tend to procrastinate, we want to be sure not to use the **awaiting** step as an excuse for inaction. We need to be conscious about when to patiently wait and when to stop waiting and take action, which is the final step.

The **acting** or action step is when we conduct ourselves in a new way. We act with clear intention. This can occur very quickly—within moments of our initial awareness, or there can be a long span of time between our awareness and our ability to act in a new way.

I think it may be valuable for you to accept your feelings, then ask the question, "How do I want to do myself?" and await. Just be curious and open up.

Tom: Open up to what?

Jake: Open up to yourself. Say, "This is what I do to myself; I anger myself and defy myself." If you accept this is what you are doing to yourself, then ask, "Is this how I want to use my personal energy? How would I like to conduct myself?" Once you open up to your perceptions, your thoughts, and your feelings you may find that you reorganize yourself in some new ways.

Tom: "Defying myself" is an interesting twist, isn't it?

Jake: Yeah, it is.

Tom: It seems somewhat paradoxical that accepting myself will lead to growth and change.

Jake: When we don't accept ourselves, we tend to become rigid. We tighten and constrict, which inhibits the process of growth and even our healing. When we're accepting, we become more fluid, softer, more malleable, and change is more likely. I observe people growing and changing much more significantly when they accept wherever they are as their starting point.

I often help myself with the image of a river. The left bank of the river represents rigidity and the right bank represents chaos. These two states—rigidity and chaos—explain all emotional and mental turmoil. We're either too rigid or too chaotic.

The solution is to flow down the river. I call it the river of integration. When we are truly integrated, which results from going through these five steps of growth, we **re**gain a sense of balance and flow in our lives.

Tom: I assume that when I use words like "defiant" to describe myself, that means I'm on the left bank.

Jake: Absolutely.

Tom: When I alter my words from "being defiant" to "defying myself," it's really interesting in ways I can't explain.

Jake: This is an example of how powerful language is. If we change the way we use language we can change our lives...and the world.

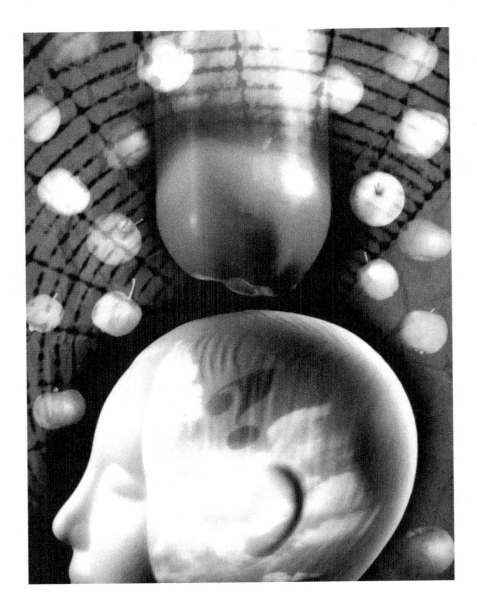

CHAPTER 7

Use Language to Turn On and Off
Different Parts of Your Brain

I was sitting at my desk looking at a photograph of Tom. Before he got sick I didn't have a picture of him on my desk. As I looked at the picture, a series of images ran through my mind, as if each one captured what Tom looked like in each decade of his life. A long-haired teenager, a young man in college—with his first serious girlfriend, a businessman in his thirties—driving sports cars, a father in his forties—mowing the lawn during the weekends, and now in his fifties—searching for meaning. These fleeting images reminded me of how quickly we travel through our lives. I wanted very much to actually see him alive as an old man.

Tom: Why do you have so much faith that changing our language can change our lives?

Jake: Because I've seen it happen time and again. And when I think about language, I view it as being made up of three dialects. The "I-dialect" describes our inner world—our world of thoughts, feelings, and perceptions. The "we-dialect" is used to make shared agreements with other people. And the "it-dialect" is the language of science and measurement.

I'll draw a quick diagram:

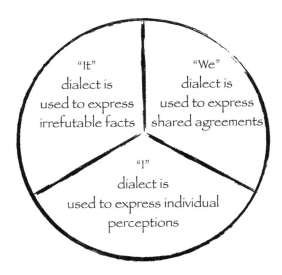

In our conversation I want to focus on the I-dialect, which is the appropriate place to use **ReSpeak**. When describing our inner worlds, for the most part, we avoid using the it-dialect because we're not talking about facts. And we avoid using the we-dialect unless we're creating agreements with other people. These distinctions show how complex our language is.

Language is our primary way to connect with other people, to reason, to introspect. It's how we make and convey meaning. If we change the way we use language, we can change the meaning in our lives. What I find exciting is that language and the way we make meaning are malleable.

Tom: Which is malleable, meaning or language?

Jake: Both. To me, they're two sides of the same coin. I use language to create meaning. If I vary my use of language I vary the meaning that I create for myself. So if I use language in a particular way—such as **ReSpeak**—I can elevate my consciousness as a result of the way I choose to speak.

Tom: But not everything is subject to interpretation. There are some things that are just the way they are. They really happen and that's indisputable. My mind goes to an event like 9/11.

Jake: 9/11 is a good example; I'm not saying that the event didn't happen, but rather that the meaning we ascribe to the event varies from person to person. That event happened, and then we each made meaning of that event in our own way. Some people made meaning of it by taking a vow to live life more fully and not take their loved ones for granted. Some people made meaning of the same event by signing up for the armed forces so that they could exact revenge on the enemy.

Tom: Or in order to protect their country and loved ones.

Jake: Absolutely. And some people made meaning of that event by holing up, not going out in the world because they feared the world had become a dangerous place. Others made meaning of that event by moving out of New York City and creating a rural lifestyle in which they felt safer. Some people moved to New York City to participate in the rebuilding and to make a personal statement that they were not going to be intimidated. Still others made meaning of that event by recommitting themselves to the jihad against America.

Tom: You're talking about people's behaviors, the actions they took, the different responses they had to the event.

Jake: Yes. We take action in our lives based upon how we assign meaning to things.

Tom: This has to do with your earlier comments about our personal filters and how they affect the way we make meaning.

Jake: They do, yes. And we can be more aware of our filters and we can **re**evaluate them. But if we were to change one thing to bring about the greatest shift in consciousness, I would suggest that we limit our use of dualistic language.

Tom: Define dualistic language.

Jake: A language is dualistic when it labels things as being either A or B—good or bad. This is the root cause of so many of our problems because, as soon as we make other people or ourselves bad, this judgment results in alienation and conflict.

Tom: But this is a part of life. Some things are good and some are bad.

Jake: Part of the brain interprets the world in that way. From that perspective, yes, some things are good and some are bad. Another part of the brain interprets events in a much more sophisticated manner. **Re**Speak does this and also keeps us from reducing people or things to being labeled as good or bad.

Tom: I have a heightened curiosity these days about the brain, so tell me exactly what you mean.

Jake: Okay. Different parts of the brain process information in different ways. In the oldest, most primitive part we process information in a dualistic way. Whatever we encounter we view as either friend or foe. When we label something as foe, this judgment stimulates fear. Our instinctual response is: fight, flight, or freeze because the intention of our primitive brain is to protect our physical body to make sure we survive.

When I feel threatened my sacrum clenches, my body stiffens, and I prepare to kill or run away from whatever threatens me. This is an instinctive, visceral reaction. I'm unaware of any thoughts.

The newer part of the brain is the neocortex. It can process information in a dualistic way, but its tendency and greatest strength is to process in a pluralistic manner. This means that instead of seeing just two meanings—friend or foe—it sees plural meanings. This part of the brain, which I call the modern brain, is a meaning-making machine. This part of the brain is curious and creative. Everything is open to interpretation. The modern brain recognizes everything as changing, flowing, organic, and arbitrary.

Tom: Two different worlds.

Jake: They're completely different. And they're both valuable and necessary. The world of the primitive brain is concrete and sensual. Everything is immediate and present, living in the now. The primitive brain needs to be present so that it can perform its main task, which is to detect any threat and respond appropriately. Because it needs to respond rapidly, there's no time for abstract thought processes. It responds instinctually.

The primitive brain senses the essence of situations. It knows how to detect the raw internal states of other mammals, including deep emotions and physiological rhythms of another being. These emotions and rhythms don't require words to be understood—they're universal. All over the world certain facial expressions that convey fear, sadness, and happiness are the same. Because of the universality of our raw emotions we can receive the depth of another person, even people who differ from us. With my primitive brain, I can feel you, but I can't explain you.

The modern brain lives in another realm—an alternative realm. The world of the modern brain is abstract, conceptual, full of imagination and fueled by thought. This is the part of the brain we use to solve complex problems, to make fine distinctions, to assign meaning to events. We use it for engineering, architecture, and politics. We use this part of the brain to navigate and negotiate the world of meaning.

Tom: But aren't both parts of the brain active all the time? I don't think we can selectively turn down the volume in one part and turn up the volume in another part of the brain.

Jake: Oh, yes we can. We do it all the time. We just don't always do this intentionally but we can. We can use language to regulate our brains. Using language in different ways stimulates different regions of the brain.

Tom: But we are who we are, especially after fifty or sixty years. How much change can we affect by altering the way we use language?

Jake: A great deal. But I hear you asking if we can change who we are by changing the way we use language. So let's talk about who we are.

CHAPTER 8

A Case of Mistaken Identity: Who Are You?

I heard Tom asking, "Can we really change?" The question applied directly to us. He and I had been stuck in our pattern of relating with one another for so many years. I hoped we could find a new way to speak to one another. His health crisis had catapulted us into another reality. I was experiencing empathy and openness toward my brother in a way that was new for me. While I was glad for this change in our relationship, I was deeply disappointed in myself for requiring such a shocking wake-up call.

Jake: How are you doing? Can we talk about what's going on for you?

Tom: Not right now. Maybe later. I'm actually curious to talk about the idea of "who we are," it's something I'm thinking a lot about.

Jake: Sure, let's talk about it.

Tom: Go ahead, tell me who you are.

Jake: I think of each of us as having an Identity. I see our Identity as our own creation, a narrative that we take with us wherever we go. Identity changes, evolving fluidly and dynamically when we allow this to happen. The resilience of Identity shows us the brilliance of this extraordinary human creation. As long as I don't get too attached to my story, my Identity continuously morphs, adapts, and integrates while serving as a temporary but necessary handhold.

No matter what we do, with few exceptions, the nature of Identity cannot be destroyed. If we deflate ourselves, we can re-inflate ourselves. If we wound ourselves, we can heal ourselves. If we make mistakes, we can learn. If we lose ourselves, we can find ourselves. If we are without meaning, we can create new meaning. Whatever happens to us, we grow until we die. When Nietzsche, the German philosopher, said, "Anything that does not kill me will make me stronger," I imagine he was talking about Identity.

Tom: This is another of your radical ideas.

Jake: This is my particular slant on something that several philosophers have explored. Buddhism suggests that there is a continuum of consciousness, but that there is no solid, permanent self anywhere in that continuum.

Tom: And you agree?

Jake: I don't pretend to know much about the continuum of consciousness beyond this lifetime. But during our lives, we lack a solid or permanent Identity. I think this is why Buddhism advocates "no self," and why I advocate an ever-changing, ever-evolving self, which is how I view Identity.

I believe that Identity is necessary because we need something to hold onto; the key is not to hold on too tightly. Imagine a jungle gym like we had on the school playground. It included a horizontal ladder and to get from one end to the other you would hold one crossbar with one hand and reach for the next crossbar with your other hand. To move along, you would alternate holding with one hand, letting go and reaching forward with the other hand.

This is kind of how I think about Identity, something to hold on to, but we keep letting go and moving forward. And instead of the ladder being horizontal, I think of it as rising up, representing an ever-higher level of consciousness.

Tom: But you don't believe in the idea of "no self"?

Jake: My sense is that "no self" is another way of saying "no fixed self." We need some way to define ourselves, to say, "This is me right now, these are my boundaries, my values, my needs. I will change and evolve, but this is me now." My focus is on how we develop a healthy Identity. One key to this is to loosen our attachments to our idea of who we are, and **Re**ology makes this easier to do.

Tom: How do you arrive at these ideas?

Jake: In part, from my own experiences. My Identity has evolved. I've gone through things that I was sure I could not survive, but I did. When I emerged on the other side, I was different. I'd become stronger, or softer, or sadder. I'd matured and became more realistic and wiser. I developed empathy and understanding.

In addition to my own life experiences, I've worked with hundreds of people who have demonstrated the resilience of their Identity. I've been with people who've suffered terrible tragedies. The nature of their Identity does not die or dissolve —it expands and evolves.

I worked with a woman who, in an alcoholic rage, murdered her two-year-old daughter. This woman served her prison sentence and came to me for therapy after she got out. She was a tough lady, at least on the outside. She transformed the nature of her Identity as a result of her experiences. Eventually, she became a fearless counselor. She knew grief, she knew guilt, she knew horror. And she knew how to survive and heal.

Tom: I actually can't imagine what that would be like. But I get your point that people are incredibly resilient. And maybe you're right, maybe our Identity is indestructible, but that's not how people act. I think most people are fundamentally insecure. I know some incredibly successful people, but in almost every case, there's a basic insecurity. It manifests in weird ways—sometimes the most powerful people will fight over the littlest things or need to be right when it shouldn't matter.

Jake: I completely agree with you. We are insecure but not because there is something wrong with us. Insecurity is just part of the way we're wired. If people understood this, they wouldn't get defensive about feeling insecure.

Tom: Are you saying it's biological, not psychological?

Jake: There is a psychological dimension, which relates to our self-esteem—lower self-esteem equates with greater insecurity —but even when we have good self-esteem we experience insecurity. This has to do with the way we're hardwired. I've thought about this for a long time and I actually think I may have uncovered a flaw in our evolutionary process.

Tom: You crack me up.

Jake: Why, what's so funny?

Tom: I don't know; you take all of this so seriously. I thought you worked with people to help them get along better, but you've developed your own theories about evolution.

Jake: I'm trying to find the key to bring about radical transformation in people's lives. If we really understand the—

Tom: I'm not being critical. I think it's great. You're passionate about this stuff. Go on. I want to hear about the flaw in evolution. I just had no idea you thought so much about this stuff, but it explains a lot about you. I've often wondered what was going on in your mind.

Jake: When I think about evolution, it includes both the evolution of our species as well as our individual evolution. I imagine our individual evolution is a microcosm of our evolution as a species.

For example, as a species we developed complex language and that dramatically altered our consciousness. The same thing happens for us individually; when as infants we develop complex language, we dramatically alter our consciousness. So when I talk about evolution, I'm talking about both our species and us as individuals.

My personal idea about human evolution is that our neocortex —the modern brain—developed in response to our awareness of time. Before we had any awareness of time, we were only aware of the present moment. At that stage in our development, the main distinction we needed to make when we encountered someone or something was whether it was friend or foe. Our primitive brain is designed to handle that task.

But as we evolved, we became aware of other aspects of time: the past and the future. This gave us a survival advantage. Remembering the past helped us to learn how to avoid mistakes and take advantage of successes. Anticipating the future helped us to prepare.

But life became exponentially more complex as our awareness extended beyond the present moment. And I imagine that this change brought about one of the greatest leaps in our evolution —complex language. We needed complex language so that we could effectively communicate in a more complex world that included past, present, and future. You can sense this huge leap forward when an infant learns to use language.

Tom: Yeah, it's a whole new world when that happens.

Jake: And this change—the development of our neocortex—is a double-edged sword; it provides enormous benefits, but there are side effects. One of which is that we experience insecurity and anxiety. Our anxiety arises because as we travel the corridors of time, living in our memories of the past and our fantasies of the future, we're no longer fully present. If we're not fully present, we often don't read situations accurately. When we don't read situations accurately, we're living in some degree of distortion, which means that our responses are less likely to be appropriate. Not being fully in the present moment is one cause for feeling insecure and anxious.

Another cause of our insecurity and anxiety is that, as we become aware of time, we become aware of uncertainty. With our newly-developed language skills we fantasize all sorts of possibilities. We anticipate the best and worst of futures. We spend a lot of time rehearsing or worrying about what may go wrong. We realize that life is a roll of the dice—we're not in total control.

In addition to not being fully present and becoming aware of uncertainty, with the development of our modern brains, we also become aware of our impermanence. We know we're going to die. In most cultures, this is cause for more insecurity and anxiety. So, although our modern brains provide significant survival advantages, they also generate a great deal of existential angst.

This brings us to what I see as a flaw in evolution, which is—

Tom: Before you go on I want to know how to deal with existential angst. A few minutes ago you asked me how I'm doing. Well, this is what I'm dealing with. What's happening for me now is pretty scary and is life-threatening. It's not just my Identity that's threatened; it's also my life. So how does one deal with this kind of angst?

Jake: I know for you this isn't about some theory. So let's talk about it in really practical terms. One key, maybe the most significant, in dealing with this angst is to live in the present because when we're fully present we aren't anxious. We can use our modern brains to help us be more present by asking the question, "What's actually happening now? Right now." When I become really present, I no longer worry about what may happen tomorrow; I'm just fully here with you now. And if I use **Re**Speak, I don't label what's happening now as "good" or "bad." This helps me accept whatever is happening now.

Tom: I can do that and you're right, it helps. But I can't stay here because, as you just said, my modern brain wanders all over the place.

Jake: And to varying degrees it will do that. So the other part of reducing existential anxiety is to accept the uncertainty of life and mortality.

Tom: It's too scary, too much to ask.

Jake: Do you want me to translate what you just said into **Re**Speak?

Tom: Sure.

Jake: I scare myself, and I ask too much of myself.

Tom: Probably all true.

Jake: Do you help yourself with the translation into **Re**Speak?

Tom: I connect more with how I feel, but I'm not sure I want to. That's my point; I don't want to accept death.

Jake: Just consider this idea. If we don't deny death, if we accept that death is inevitable for all of us, and as a result we live a more conscious life, aren't we more likely to feel better about the life we live? If I'm conscious of my mortality—aware that I only have so much time here, whether five months or fifty years—I don't want to waste precious time; I feel compelled to do certain things.

Tom: Like what?

Jake: I want to connect with the people I love. I want to clear up any unfinished business so that I leave a healthy emotional footprint. I want to express myself to certain people. I want the people I love to witness me and I want to witness them.

Here's the bottom line: if I live consciously, I attend to the things that are most meaningful to me. Living this way helps me accept my death. My focus is on living, not dying, but my awareness of death affects the way I live.

Tom: Yes, I agree with what you're saying.

Jake: There's one more piece in this existential puzzle: learning to accept uncertainty. This is much easier to do if we believe— as I do—that Identity is ever evolving. When I see myself in this way—constantly evolving—I'm less resistant to changes in my life because I realize that everything is temporary. I loosen my grip and stop holding so tightly onto my idea of myself.

For me, the most difficult thing to face is the death of people I love. But I help myself a great deal when I think that "I" will evolve in response to everything that happens in my life...even the death of my loved ones.

So I guess I'm saying a few things. Being present is the best way I know to reduce anxiety. Living my life fully and consciously is the best way I know to deal with anxiety about my own death. And believing "I" will evolve in response to everything that happens, even the worst things, is the best way I know to deal with my anxiety about any tragedy that I survive.

Tom: Realistically, I'm facing the loss of my life, not just my Identity. When I die my Identity dies right along with my body.

Jake: Maybe. But not in the hearts and minds of other people. Your Identity-in-them lives on. You will live on in me and in your kids, and others. At this point, you still have a chance to play a role in shaping the Identity that others hold of you. You have a chance to **re**-right your life.

Tom: Hence the title of your book?

Jake: Yes. We all have a chance to **re**-right our lives. I believe that if we pay really close attention we almost always know what's right for us. But for various reasons, we deviate, we take wrong turns. And the further we get away from living our unique lives—and the longer we stay away—the more we suffer.

The answer is to re-right our lives, come back to what we know is right for us. **Re**align ourselves. Conduct ourselves in ways so that we make ourselves proud.

Tom: And never too late?

Jake: I don't think so. We just finished conducting one of our retreats in Mexico. We had a guy attend—who was also a friend of ours—who only has six months to live. He came to the retreat and worked on two unresolved issues. By the time he left he said, "I'm right with myself, I'm actually happy, and I'm ready to die."

Tom: How old is he?

Jake: Sixty-eight. Too young. But he's going to do this final thing really well.

And when we die, who knows what happens to our actual Identity? Likely, it just keeps on changing as it merges with the rest of the universe.

Tom: Is that what you believe?

Jake: I don't know. I hope that's what happens.

Tom: Me too.

CHAPTER 9

A Flaw in Evolution

My sense of Tom was that he had always lived with a great deal of certainty. He was confident, competitive, and he usually got what he wanted. So I imagined that our conversation about uncertainty was particularly challenging. More significantly, his illness created uncertainty that was foreign to him.

I wanted to check in with him, to hear how he was doing, but he seemed reluctant to talk about himself.

Jake: What do you think? Does any of this help?

Tom: It's simmering…I'm simmering. I'm thinking about it all. I comfort myself with your idea that I can shape the Identity I leave behind in the hearts and minds of other people. I'm certain I can re-right my life, not my past, but my present.

I interrupted you earlier when you started talking about a flaw in evolution.

Jake: I was saying that I believe the modern brain—which is the cause of most of our anxiety—created our Identities to quell our anxiety. Once we became aware of uncertainty and impermanence, we needed something to hold onto. Identity provides us with a sense of continuity, not permanence, but continuity. I'm convinced that's why the modern brain created Identity, to give us the experience of continuity. Continuity is comforting.

And this gets us to what I believe is a flaw in evolution—we often make a mistake when we think of Identity the same way we think of the physical body. We act as if our Identities can be destroyed, just like our bodies can be destroyed. But Identity is a mental construct, and as long as we're alive, our Identities endure. We don't need to be highly reactive when we perceive our Identities to be threatened. We don't need to react to words as if they are swords.

We use the criteria of our primitive brains—the criteria of "Do I feel safe or not?"—to evaluate the lives we construct with our modern brains. We evaluate too many things in terms of being good or bad, right or wrong, friend or foe. These questions, these criteria stimulate the primitive brain—not to the point of fear—but just enough so that we get stuck in a perpetual cycle of anxiety. But do you see how we're asking the wrong questions, inside the wrong paradigm, using the wrong criteria? These criteria don't apply to our Identities. They are way too limiting.

To break this cycle we need to step outside of the primitive brain's dualistic gestalt, and see our lives through a pluralistic gestalt.

Tom: What does that mean?

Jake: When we view our lives through a pluralistic gestalt we see possibilities, we feel our potential that goes beyond just "safe or not safe." We know that we—our Identities—are fundamentally safe, so we look for ways to express ourselves, to nurture our possibilities, and to transform our previous limitations. Our modern brains are fully capable of this. Only when we engage our modern brains can we see the totality of situations—the complexity. We can see that what's best for one person may not be what's best for ourselves. With a broadened perspective, we have more freedom and more choices in terms of how we author our lives. We can **re**-right our life in a way that's best for us. When we live our lives in ways where we fully honor and appreciate ourselves, we become less concerned about uncertainty and mortality.

Tom: It's funny that when I listen to you, part of me wants to insist that certain things just are the way they are. I feel my attachment to certain ideas I have about myself. But another part of me recognizes the freedom that comes from letting go or loosening up.

Jake: One of our greatest challenges is loosening and expanding our sense of who we are. Most of us have such limited and fixed ideas about ourselves. As you said, we get attached. We hold on tightly. We defend our Identities as if they were our physical bodies. We rely on the primitive brain tactics of fighting, fleeing and freezing. When we execute these tactics with our modern brains, we fight with words, we flee by emotionally abandoning others and ourselves, and we freeze by victimizing and paralyzing ourselves with fear. But we don't need to. If we embrace our Identities as ever evolving then we don't need to fight, flee, or freeze.

I worked with a woman who came to see me because she thought she was dying, even though the doctors could not find any physical cause for her concerns. She stopped doing the things in her life that needed to be done. She said her life felt as if it were spiraling out of control. I asked her when the feelings began and she said, "Shortly after my sister died, which was four months ago."

I asked, "How have you responded to your sister's death?"

She explained, "I'm shocked that I'm okay. My entire life I thought that when my sister died, I would die for sure. She's the only person left from my original family. Now there is no one left but me."

I said, "It sounds to me like part of you did die when your sister died. Not only did you lose someone you were deeply connected to, but you lost your belief that when she died you would die."

She said, "Well, I'm pretty much lost. I'm not functioning well at all. I might as well have died."

I gently pointed out the obvious. "But you didn't die. I think this may be why you're so disoriented. You held this idea about yourself for your entire life. You thought that when your sister died, you would die. This was part of your Identity. But when your sister died you didn't die. This means you are not exactly who you thought you were. Maybe now you can change your ideas about yourself?"

Three days later this woman called me to say, "As a result of our session I feel like I opened the door to a new room in my mind and closed the door to an old room. I think you were right, the only thing that was dying since my sister died was my idea that I couldn't live without my sister." The transformation this woman experienced was at an Identity level.

Tom: Is that what you mean by having an ever evolving Identity?

Jake: Yes, she allowed her Identity to evolve. In her particular case, she required an enormous event to bring this about, but that's not always necessary. Small changes in Identity can occur all the time if we don't resist.

I want to tell you about an experience I had when I was in my early twenties. I don't know if you remember when I went to Virginia for a training program to learn about group dynamics?

Tom: No, I didn't know you did that.

Jake: It was a great experience. There were seventy to eighty students, and we worked in small groups of twelve. The first group I was in included a big, tough-looking man from Washington, D.C.—very intimidating—and a small woman who was a nun named Mary. She had only one arm and she was struggling with a terminal illness. During one of our early sessions this big guy was giving the little nun a really hard time.

He was unloading on her, venting his frustrations about how righteous religious people can be. I piped up and told him that he seemed pretty righteous himself, and if he wanted to pick on someone, he should find someone his own size. I felt great defending the little nun who seemed so helpless. When I was done speaking my mind, the little nun got my attention by touching my arm. I looked down at her and she said, "Why don't you mind your own fucking business?"

All my preconceptions about her, and nuns, and small women, and people with disabilities, and people with terminal illness, and nuns using the word "fuck" were shattered. My beliefs shifted. I was forever different. She was forever different in my mind. My idea of being a savior was different. My Identity expanded in that moment as a result of the little nun, Mary, revealing herself.

Tom: That's a great story, Jake.

Jake: I haven't thought about that experience for a long time, but I think it's a good example of the larger point I'm trying to make. I thought that this big intimidating guy was harming Mary. I was trying to defend her as if she were under physical attack. But Mary knew better. She knew her Identity was durable because she had survived so much in her life. She didn't feel herself to be in danger and she didn't need me to protect her Identity.

Tom: Earlier, I asked you about the solution to our existential angst. It seems you're saying the answer is to accept these things that we generally find uncomfortable: uncertainty and death.

Jake: Yes, and to do so is easier if we live in the present and if we recognize the flexibility and resiliency of our Identities. We adapt and grow until we die—continuously renewing ourselves.

Tom: Or we don't.

Jake: I guess that's up to each of us.

Tom: My Identity has changed since I got this tumor. I never used to get tired or need to rest, but now I do, so let's take a break for a while.

Jake: All right, let me know when you feel like continuing.

It was so odd to hear Tom say he was tired. I'd always known him to have such a strong physical constitution. As a result of his illness, he seemed completely accepting that he had certain limits. This made him seem more human to me. In some way, I liked him better. I felt terrible thinking I liked him better when he was sick, but I did find it easier to relate with him. Adversity can be revealing. I played a mind game with myself, asking, "Would I rather he never got sick and that we never had this special time together? Or, would I rather that he had his health but we remain strangers?"

What I really wanted was for him to be healthy and for us to learn to connect just like we were now. But if I had to choose one or the other, I'd choose for him to be healthy.

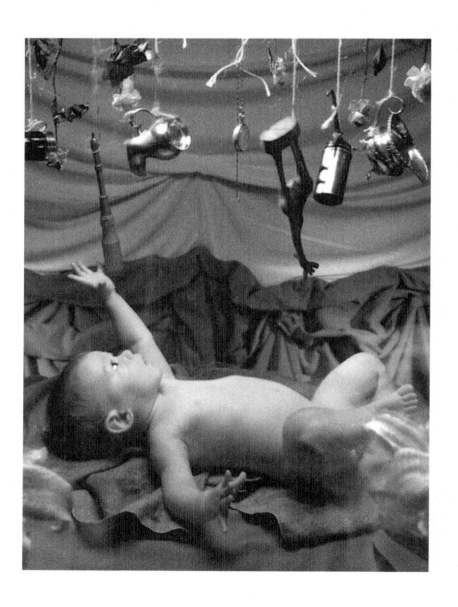

CHAPTER 10

All of You Is Who You Are

I realized that my present relationship with Tom was dramatically different because the context had so severely changed. As context shifts, meaning changes. During all my adult years Tom had various habits that I was critical of. After he became ill, the same habits and behaviors didn't bother me at all. I had what felt like unlimited patience and acceptance. It was a gracious way to be with him and to be with myself.

But I'm a realist. I knew if Tom were to live through this, and I were to visit him, I might remain non-reactive to those behaviors that I had found troubling, at least for the first day of the visit. But by the second day or the third, or after a month, I would start to reassert my boundaries and preferences. I wasn't critical of myself for this; I accept that as the context of our lives is altered, our boundaries and tolerances are altered. But I decided that I wanted to hold a larger perspective as I moved forward in my life, a perspective that would eliminate pettiness and foster bigheartedness.

When we continued our conversation I sensed that Tom had been wrestling with some of the things we had previously talked about.

Tom: You have a lot of intriguing ideas. I guess I should say, I intrigue myself with your ideas. Your ideas seem very practical, which I appreciate. Sometimes I hear thoughtful people talk, or I've read philosophers who write about the need to overcome duality and the need to transcend our ego. These ideas seem less practical to me, but I'm curious to know what you think.

Jake: My sense is that many of my ideas are in alignment with several of the great philosophers. However, some of their ideas get misconstrued as they travel from one source to another. I think that's happened around the topics of both duality and ego. Some people interpret the great teachers—like Buddha—as saying that duality is an illusion, but according to what I've read, it's a misconception that Buddhism views duality solely as an illusion or as a defect. My understanding is that Buddha viewed duality as one aspect of human experience, a necessary, but limited perspective, which is the same thing I'm saying.

As soon as I make the distinction between "self" and "other," I've created duality. And this is what human beings do. I know many people say that duality is an illusion, that we're not separate, that we're all connected. They talk about a state of being that is empty of self-consciousness, a state where the self is one with all. Meditation is often used as a vehicle to reach this state. And yet, when we're going about our life, generally we are not in that meditative state—which for most of us isn't easy to attain even sitting in meditation—and we often experience ourselves as separate.

And I think it's ironic when people say that duality is a defect. Saying "duality is wrong or bad" is being dualistic. And my point is that duality is not wrong or right, it's just part of the human experience, a significant part. And because of that, I want us to learn to constructively work with duality when we must and to minimize it when we can so that we don't unnecessarily limit ourselves.

There are times when we must distinguish between "self" and "other"—we must acknowledge our separateness. This is part of our survival mechanism. Our immune system does this all the time; it protects us with its ability to recognize "self" and "not

94

self." We need to be able to identify any "foe" so that we will take the appropriate actions.

Another example is that when we are young infants, we grow apart from our mother and learn that we are separate from her —our body is separate from hers, our emotions are separate from hers, and our mind is separate from hers. These are all necessary steps toward psychological health.

If we don't experience our physical selves as separate, we'll suffer from severe confusion later in life. If we don't experience our emotional selves as separate, we'll struggle with narcissism and feeling overwhelmed later in life. If we don't experience our mental selves as separate, later on we'll struggle with inner conflicts. These experiences of separation are essential to our mental health.

Tom: It seems to me that people want to believe that duality is an illusion.

Jake: Sure, because it's comforting to think that we're all one, all connected.

Tom: Do you have any comfort to offer to these people?

Jake: I comfort myself by acknowledging my experience, not by denying it. I experience myself as separate and alone, not all the time, but much of the time. So I start from there. I ground myself by acknowledging my experience.

I comfort myself when I step into the **Re**ology worldview, which is based on respecting our differences. When I do this I stop alienating myself from people who are different from me; in part, because I recognize that—even though we have differences —we share certain things in common. One of the things we share is that we are together in our aloneness. I comfort myself with this awareness.

When I respect our differences I stop diminishing myself by comparing myself with others, and I stop diminishing others; instead I simply accept that we're different.

I comfort myself with the idea that **Re**ology asks me to take responsibility for my emotional footprint, because when I do that, I like myself better, so I'm more okay with being alone. I like my own company.

Tom: What I hear you saying is that you work with your experience of duality instead of trying to overcome it.

Jake: Yes. That's true, but I also use **Re**Speak as a way to diminish, not eliminate, but diminish making dualistic distinctions. Instead of seeing things as right or wrong, I make pluralistic distinctions—I see multiple points of view.

Tom: Okay, this is helpful.

Jake: I help myself.

Tom: Right, I help myself. And what do you think about the need to transcend our egos?

Jake: "Transcend" means to go beyond. I concern myself with the idea of transcending our egos because I don't want to encourage people to separate from themselves. I believe that separating or dissociating from parts of ourselves—including our egos—is risky. If we do separate from parts of ourselves we create a divided self. Other than a few exceptions I can think of, creating a divided self will limit our growth. I've experienced this in my own life and I've observed many clients trying to discard, ignore, and minimize parts of themselves. When we create distance from parts of ourselves that we don't like, we diminish our health. We become anxious and defensive because we fear that the discarded parts will reemerge. As soon as we accept these parts and integrate them, we become healthier. Accepting all aspects of ourselves is how we make ourselves whole.

Tom: But isn't our ego the basis for many of our petty, selfish desires?

Jake: I see the word "ego" as a symbol for the conscious self. Having an ego doesn't automatically mean I'm petty or selfish. My ego is a reflection of my state of consciousness. I want to elevate my consciousness so that I can act wisely and respond appropriately to events in my life. As I elevate my consciousness, the expression of my ego evolves. Just because I have an ego, that doesn't make me egotistical.

I encourage people to live with their egos, appreciate their egos, and take full responsibility for their egos, which I believe takes a long time. Along the way, we begin to recognize that our egos are not static or permanent, but ever changing. We begin to lessen our attachment to our stories as we mature ourselves. Can we get to a place of no ego? I don't know, but I see too many people prematurely striving for that. I've heard this referred to as "spiritual bypassing." When this happens we find ourselves looking so far down the road that we stumble over the pebble immediately in front of us.

Tom: You don't feel limited by your ego?

Jake: I don't. I limit myself by my own immaturity, but I don't blame my ego for that. I think of my ego or my Identity as a way I have of organizing myself so that I can make sense of the world. I see us all doing this. We need to make sense of the world in ways that help us minimize our anxiety. We rely on our Identities to offer ourselves certainty and a frame of reference.

As we mature and our consciousness develops, we will grow beyond an exclusively egocentric perspective. We'll develop an ethnocentric perspective, which means a concern for our families and our tribes. And if our growth continues, eventually we'll develop a world-centric perspective, which means a concern and interest for all people—even those that we once didn't recognize as belonging to our tribes. But all this growth is predicated upon having a healthy ego. We never get rid of our egos or other parts of ourselves; we just build upon ourselves.

Tom: I think you're saying that our attempts to distance ourselves from our egos or any parts of ourselves we don't like, like our inauthentic self, is a mistake.

Jake: No, that's just my point. There is no inauthentic self! We are all of who we are, including our self-deceptions, our lies about our mortality, and our immaturity. These are all aspects of us. To suggest that these aspects are the false self and that the true self is glorious, honest, and pure as virgin snow, well, this just fosters more judgment about not being good enough. As a result of thinking we're not okay we're motivated to hide the aspects of ourselves that are unattractive. These are the aspects that people talk about as "false." And we're less likely to take responsibility for the aspects of us that we label as "false." It's so easy to say, "Well, that wasn't my real self, that was my false self." I see this when I do couples counseling, and the man turns to his wife and says, "Honey, when I said, 'No, I don't want to understand why you feel that way,' I wasn't speaking from my heart; please ignore that." This is like saying I wasn't speaking from my true self, my authentic self, my good self, so please disregard what I said.

Tom: And you don't want her to disregard what he said?

Jake: Of course not. First of all, what he said is a comment about him, not about her. But whatever he said, it is part of him and part of the way this couple relates to one another. I want him to own that part of himself.

Tom: So what should he say?

Jake: Just don't deny yourself. Don't say, "It wasn't really me talking." I would encourage the couple to be curious about what the husband was saying. Where do his attitudes and corresponding beliefs come from? If he's not talking from his heart, what stops him? What part of him is doing the talking? I want him to take responsibility for that part, not excuse it and brush it aside. I want him to accept this part of himself and integrate it, so that he stops trying to avoid it. Trying to avoid parts of himself will only result in those parts cropping up in unconscious ways at some future point in time. I'm trying to do away with the distinction of good self and bad self, a true self and a false self, an authentic self and an inauthentic self. I don't find these dualistic distinctions helpful. They only exacerbate our anxiety about being seen as bad, false, or inauthentic.

Tom: This is really a very different approach from anything I've heard before. It seems like there's nowhere to hide.

Jake: There's no reason to hide.

Tom: But we do hide.

Jake: And by hiding, we inhibit our growth. All the ways we hide and repress are the most significant obstacles to living a healthy life. And they are rampant, even epidemic.

CHAPTER 11

The Source of Your Exhaustion

When I was a young teenager, Tom and I traveled with our sister, Lizabeth, to Tuckerman's Ravine in the White Mountain National Forest. Tuckerman's was famous for having so much snow that hardy skiers would go there to ski in late spring, even early summer, if they were willing to hike six miles round-trip to the base camp. From the base camp, those who chose to do so would push on to ascend the steep slopes above the base camp. Hiking up the slope, with skis on your back, limited most people to one or possibly two runs a day.

During the middle of our trip I got quite sick, to the point that I was unable to walk back down the trail. My sister and her boyfriend ended up accompanying me down the trail in a Snowcat, and then driving me five hours back home. I was embarrassed to have to be taken care of, even though I was sick. I remember worrying about what Tom thought of me. I didn't want him to see me as frail. This experience was one of many that contributed to me wanting to hide any sense of weakness.

Tom: "Rampant and epidemic"? That's pretty strong language.

Jake: Do you remember we talked about the Greek definition of the word "phenomenal"?

Tom: To reveal oneself.

Jake: If we use that definition, then we can't live a phenomenal life if we hide. Hiding is the greatest obstacle to living a phenomenal life. When we hide aspects of ourselves we live partial lives. We don't get to deeply know ourselves and we don't allow others to deeply know us. We minimize our potential for intimacy.

Tom: I thought that one of your beliefs is that I can never fully know you. So, in a way, what difference does it make if I reveal more or less of myself to you?

Jake: It's all relative. If you hide from me then I know you in a limited way. Even if I like you, but there's much you haven't shown me about yourself, you'll be anxious because you'll wonder what will happen when I discover more of you. Newly romantic couples often do this...they hold back for fear that their prospective partner will discover something he or she doesn't like. I see this as a really flawed strategy. I think you might as well put yourself out there, show up, and speak up early in a relationship—before the stakes are high—and find out if you're compatible.

If you make an effort to more fully reveal yourself to me then I can form a more complete sense of you in my mind. You're correct that I don't believe we will completely and fully know each other, but if we reveal ourselves to one another in as honest a way as we're capable of, you and I will have a vital relationship. And if we do, your affections, criticisms, concerns, and acknowledgments will be significant to me and, hopefully, mine will be significant to you. I want that with my closest people. That's part of how I make my life meaningful.

Tom: Based on how important all of this is to you, I assume that you don't hide much. But do you think you've hidden from me?

Jake: Yes, I've hidden from you. Less so in the past two or three years, but growing up, actually for the first forty years of my life, I spent a lot of time hiding. I hid from myself. Then I had an experience on my fortieth birthday in which I woke up to how much I was repressing myself. Ever since then, I fascinated myself with the power and pervasiveness of repression, and I make a strong effort not to repress. With you I still have a lot of old habits, but I'm changing them.

Tom: What happened when you turned forty?

Jake: To celebrate my fortieth birthday, Hannah and I flew to Santa Barbara for a weekend getaway. We were hanging out by the pool, thoroughly relaxed and enjoying ourselves. In the pool, we took turns, one pulling the other across the surface of the water, while the one being pulled floated on their back with their arms outstretched. When I was the one floating, my ears remained underwater, all the sounds were muffled, and my eyes were closed. I felt myself to be nowhere in particular, no time, no boundaries, and with no sense of attachment. I felt warm and comfortable. After a while, the motion of being pulled ceased and I felt myself slowly sinking, while gently being guided so that I ended up cradled in Hannah's lap, my head on her shoulder. I was in the warm water, feeling the sun shining on me, sensing that I was completely safe. I experienced myself as a child, without conscious thoughts. I felt wonderful. But at some point, I became anxious. Not afraid of any one thing but anxious about nothing in particular, nothing I could identify. The world seemed scary. I had no words to express myself, no labels. I disoriented myself with anxiety.

At some point, there was a flicker of self-consciousness and I became aware of my grown-up self, but I stayed connected with this very deep inner angst. I awakened from this trance state very slowly and allowed myself to stay in a bit of a slumber because I sensed how important this experience was. I'd never previously been so aware of this deep primal angst.

For the next couple of days I allowed myself to stay connected with my feelings. I wrote, napped, talked a bit with Hannah about my experience, and I waited, which was unusual for me. I continued to feel my deep angst, bordering on fear. I had a hard time accepting that these ancient feelings were still in me. They reminded me of feelings from my childhood, feelings I had spent a great deal of energy trying to overcome since I was very young. All those years of learning how to manage my mind! I had worked so hard to address the angst I felt as a child. But after all these efforts, including becoming a therapist, on my fortieth birthday I discovered this deep anxiety was still in me.

That's when I began to understand the power of repression. I had repressed a great deal over my forty years without knowing I was doing so. I had created a life to cover up the deeper part of me, the scared part of me, because I didn't want to risk having that part of me criticized, misunderstood, or rejected.

That's why I hid from you. I went through what might turn out to be half of my life, hiding some of the deepest parts of myself. I covered up a great deal of my very sensitive nature. I repressed those feelings. And to create safety, I disguised myself with bravado. I compensated as a way to hide. This is how repression works.

Over a period of twenty-five years, both in my life as a businessman and my life as a therapist, I conducted myself in ways to compensate for my angst. I was successful and rewarded by our culture, but I exhausted myself. Not until I grew really tired—as a result of all the energy that's required to hide—was I willing to let go of my compensating behaviors and allow the deeper aspects of myself to emerge.

Tom: And this was after your experience in the swimming pool?

Jake: Yes, but I took a little while to figure myself out. The experience in the swimming pool was when I first became aware of and fascinated with the power of repression. I just couldn't imagine anybody working any harder to overcome his or her anxiety. But that day in the pool, for many reasons, I came face to face with my existential angst.

Tom: What are the "many reasons," and what was all that fear about?

Jake: First, by the time I was forty I felt secure enough in my life that I was not afraid to look more deeply into myself. I had created enough stability: I had a solid marriage and was making a comfortable living doing work I loved. The second reason is connected with that experience in the swimming pool: lying in the water, being held, feeling safe, feeling the warmth of the sun and the connection with Hannah—all of that allowed me to go more deeply into myself.

As for your other question, "What was that fear about?" I want to reemphasize a critical distinction: fear and anxiety are fundamentally different responses coming from different parts of our brains. Fear is about a specific threat, something that we can identify and take action against. We can fight, take flight, or freeze. Our primitive brains respond to fear by taking action.

Anxiety is more complicated. Sometimes anxiety relates to a particular event—often it's something to do with our future. We may be able to identify a particular action we can take that will resolve that kind of anxiety. But there is a deeper form of anxiety that I'm more interested in—our existential angst. This deep angst is primarily a product of the modern brain. It's not about anything that we can identify; therefore, there is no clear and definitive action we can take to alleviate this anxiety.

Instead of being about something, this deep anxiety is about *not* something: *not* knowing, the unknown, the unknowable. It has to do with the uncertainty that comes from living in the abstract world of our modern brains. We make ourselves anxious in response to uncertainty and we don't have any specific action we can take. Often, our modern brain responds to anxiety by repressing that which makes us uncomfortable.

We give ourselves momentary relief, but in not dealing with the cause of our anxiety, we build a reserve, which manifests as low-level chronic anxiety.

Tom: Are you saying that we can't take action to fight our anxiety?

Jake: The idea of "fighting" anxiety is a primitive brain response, and this is often what we do—we reach for the toolbox of the primitive brain and frame things in extreme terms. This is when we become inappropriately aggressive, or we run away, or we paralyze ourselves. With all of these responses we're taking ourselves in the wrong direction because there is nothing to kill and nothing to run from.

Tom: It seems to me that we're trying to turn our anxiety into something identifiable so that we can take action to resolve it.

Jake: Yes. I see this with clients in therapy all the time. As soon as people label the cause of their anxiety, if the cause is actionable, they start to feel better.

Tom: Did you ever read Rollo May's book, *Man's Search for Himself?*

Jake: No.

Tom: It was in Dad's bookshelf. I remember a great line from that book that reminds me of what we're talking about. May said, "Anxiety seeks to become fear." That's what you're saying; we're turning our anxiety into fear so we can respond to it.

Jake: Yes, we try to turn anxiety into fear so that we can run from it or kill it. But since we can't kill our existential angst, and we can't run from it—because "it" is us—we repress it. We deny, lie, distract, confuse ourselves, and make excuses—all in an effort to alleviate our angst.

Tom: Which doesn't work very well, so what do you recommend?

Jake: I'm advocating that we use **Re**Speak as a way to stop inviting our primitive brains into conversations where they aren't needed. Instead of distracting ourselves with a primitive brain response—such as fighting—we use **Re**Speak to bring ourselves into the present and honestly reveal what we're doing to ourselves.

Tom: Is this the focus of your therapy nowadays?

Jake: Yes. As my clients learn to use **Re**Speak, their self-judgments diminish and they free themselves from unnecessary anxiety. They become more honest with themselves and with people in their lives. This leads to deeper intimacy, more congruence, and the ability to engage in deeper psychological work.

I encourage my clients to work through the deepest issues, the ones having to do with the meaning of life and acceptance of death. When they develop clarity about these issues, their existential angst diminishes.

Tom: Although you help people minimize their anxiety, you also seem to think of anxiety as a symptom—almost an opportunity—that we can take advantage of?

Jake: For the most part, yes. Anxiety is not simply to be forsaken. It's a sign that we're not right with ourselves—and an invitation to **re**-right ourselves. Anxiety is often an indication that we may be repressing something.

Tom: I'm curious if you think I repress?

Jake: I think just about everyone does. But I'd like to say a bit more about what I mean by repression, then you tell me if you think you repress.

CHAPTER 12

What Don't You Want to Know About Yourself?

I was the best man at Tom's wedding. I felt flattered that he had asked me, and also nervous because he said the best man was responsible for giving a toast. Shortly before the wedding, Tom sensed my concern about giving the toast and he suggested I use the following: "May your marriage be as long as my toast is short." I asked him if he was serious and he said, "Sure, why not?"

I disappointed myself with his suggestion because I saw the toast as a chance to say something meaningful. Tom's suggestion was clever, but it felt like an attempt to hide behind humor, which I didn't want to do.

I came up with my own toast, but it wasn't as memorable as his.

Jake: We repress whatever we anticipate will be intolerable. Different people find different things to be intolerable. Some people repress specific emotions, such as anger, but are comfortable expressing joy, while for other people it's the exact opposite. Some people repress certain kinds of thoughts, such as memories. There are people who find intimacy intolerable, so that's what they repress. We repress what we anticipate will be intolerable as a way to minimize our anxiety.

When we repress—regardless of what we repress—we squelch our life force. We use our personal energy to deny or avoid certain thoughts or feelings. Whether we do this in our interactions with other people, or in the privacy of our own minds, it's not usually the best use of our energy—certainly not over a long period of time. Repression tends to cause confusion and quash our intelligence.

I find it astonishing how really smart people fool themselves when they repress. And we do this in so many ways. Some are small ways that happen numerous times throughout the day; other forms of repression show up as major life patterns.

Tom: Give me some practical examples of what you're talking about.

Jake: Let's say you're mad at one person, but you take it out on someone else—a safe target. In this case you're hiding the target of your feelings from yourself. Or, maybe you hide the reason behind your feelings—you make up a false reason. This is called rationalization. Or you hide the source of your feelings; we do this when we project onto someone else how we're feeling or what we're thinking. Most of us do these things without even realizing we're doing them.

Tom: But it's very common for people to hide in the ways you mentioned.

Jake: And very costly. Each act of hiding seems so small in and of itself—we act as if this doesn't matter. But do you remember that equation of doubling a penny every day for twenty-eight days and you end up with over a million dollars? This is sort of like that: each time we step away from ourselves there is a cost, and the cost adds up. The ultimate cost is that we lose ourselves, we lose our health, and we lose the possibility of having truly intimate relationships.

In addition to these examples of day-to-day repression, we also establish life patterns that are based on repressing ourselves.

Doing this usually requires getting other people to collude with us, which makes it very difficult to undo these patterns.

Tom: What kind of patterns are you talking about?

Jake: One pattern involves hiding our limitations. Another pattern involves hiding our capabilities. Both tend to lead us into unhealthy relationships. When we hide our limitations, we go through the world with an expanded sense of ourselves. Our self-perception is greater than what can be supported by the evidence of our lives. The act of expanding—or over-estimating ourselves—is a way in which we make ourselves feel safer. It's a common strategy used by many overachievers. The expanded posture can be very constructive, but not when we expand too far beyond our actual capabilities.

If my self-perception is too far astray from my capabilities—as shown by the evidence of my life—then I drift into living a distorted life. I often see people do this when they start romantic relationships. We may misrepresent ourselves, for example, saying and acting as if we are comfortable with intimacy when maybe we're not. This leads to attracting potential partners who hold an expectation of us, but it's one that we can't necessarily fulfill. We end up pressuring ourselves, we hide our self-doubt and our concerns, and we make excuses when we fail to be intimate, or worse, we blame our partner. If challenged around this issue, we become defensive, which is more proof that we aren't comfortable with intimacy.

When we're extremely expanded, we expend a great deal of personal energy maintaining our illusory ideas about who we are. In the process, we have to find people to validate our illusory ideas and, in doing so, we're very likely to end up in some kind of dependent relationship. We depend upon other people to support our delusions.

On the other end of the continuum of hiding, we hide our capabilities and we contract, or shrink—we under-estimate ourselves. Again, our self-perception does not line up with the evidence of our lives.

Tom: I understand why a person would hide their limitations, but not why someone would hide their capabilities.

Jake: It's one way to avoid taking responsibility. Sometimes we feel safer when we underestimate ourselves. It's usually an unconscious strategy we use when we feel overwhelmed by demands we think we can't satisfy. Without consciously choosing to do so, psychologically we go on strike. We contract, often without complaining, because complaining invites attention. We don't want attention so much as we want to become invisible. Other times we blame our circumstances on someone else, turning ourselves into a victim. Either way, we avoid taking full responsibility for ourselves.

When we contract, we make ourselves small as a way to maintain our illusory ideas about who we are. We find people to validate our illusory ideas, and in doing so, again, we're very likely to end up in some kind of dependent relationship.

With both of these life patterns, whether we expand or contract, we misrepresent ourselves to ourselves and to other people. Both are ways of hiding. Both prevent us from allowing our full self to emerge and to live a phenomenal life in which we freely reveal who we are.

Tom: So much of what you describe seems normal to me. I see these dynamics all the time. Do you really think it's so damaging?

Jake: I do, based on my definition of health, which is responding appropriately to life events. It doesn't matter if I hide my abilities or my limitations; if I hide, I can't respond appropriately.

And you can't respond appropriately to me if I hide the true reason or cause that's behind my thoughts or feelings. So when

I hide, I inhibit our ability to connect and my possibility to learn and grow.

If I feel a certain way, but project my feelings onto you—telling you I know how you feel—how can we quickly and easily sort ourselves out? All these situations become terribly confusing because they're not based on clarity and honesty, but distortion. So, for me, as an advocate for health, I think repression is a serious problem.

Tom: It seems to me that the trickiest thing about repression is being able to identify it because we don't know what we don't know.

Jake: That's true. The key is to be deeply aware of our internal experiences. With this awareness comes a felt-sense that informs us if we're repressing something. When I experience that felt-sense, I help myself if I express myself in a way that acknowledges what I'm experiencing.

Tom: It seems tricky to me to be aware of something that is occurring outside of conscious awareness.

Jake: Repression occurs both outside of our awareness and within our awareness. When it occurs within my awareness, I know that I'm hiding some part of myself. In these situations, the first thing to do is be honest about the fact that I'm hiding —honest with myself and with other people.

Tom: Isn't that a contradiction?

Jake: No, I can be honest about the fact that I'm hiding something, but that doesn't mean I'm prepared to tell you what I'm hiding. In my experience, this kind of disclosure is very powerful.

Tom: I can see that leading to an argument about why you won't tell me the details of what's going on for you.

Jake: And I can honestly respond to you. Maybe I tell you that I'm afraid you'll be critical of me or that you'll think less of me. But now we're having an honest conversation about exactly what's going on for the two of us.

Tom: That takes a good deal of maturity, but I agree it would be more constructive than not taking responsibility for my choice to hide from you. What about my original question, which is how do we know we're hiding something when it's happening outside of our awareness?

Jake: There's the felt-sense I spoke about. We feel that something is off. Each time we repress, whether we deny, self-justify, or make excuses, we're stepping into a defensive posture, which has a certain sensation or feeling to it. It's not a "being true to myself" feeling. Sometimes, when we repress we feel excessive energy, manic or hyper. At other times there is a sense of fatigue, a draining away of our energy. When I realize I'm feeling off, but I don't know why, I stop and retrace what I've been doing to figure out when I stopped being true to myself. I have a few key questions that I ask to **re**-right myself:

"What did I say that wasn't completely honest?"

"What didn't I say that I needed to say?"

"What should I be doing, that I'm not doing?"

"What am I doing, that I shouldn't be doing?"

"What don't I want to know?"

I find these questions really helpful, especially the last one. What is it that we don't want to know?

Tom: If I don't want to know, how will I?

Jake: Try asking the question. I think you may be surprised what you learn. And remember to **re**move praise and blame.

I'm curious if all of this is helping you answer your question about whether or not you repress yourself?

Tom: I take the fifth.

Jake: I think taking the fifth is a form of repression.

Tom: At least I'm conscious of it. I do understand what you're saying about the ways we hide and how common this is. I also understand that when we misrepresent ourselves and other people go along with us—they don't challenge us—we're more likely to end up dependent on those people. They validate our lies.

Jake: And the answer is so simple.

CHAPTER 13

Honesty Leads to Sanity

During the winter when we built my log home I applied for admission at Middlebury College. It was a long shot that I'd get in because I'd dropped out of high school. The day my letter arrived from Middlebury, Tom and I were on our way to a meeting at the local bank. Our plan was to borrow some money so that we could buy an old mill and convert it to a bar/restaurant that I'd manage while going to school.

We were sitting together in my truck, and Tom asked, "Are you going to open it?" I said, "In a minute. Why don't you go ahead and I'll catch up with you." I waited a minute, opened the letter, and was ecstatic to find out I'd been accepted. I took a couple of minutes to revel in my surprise, then headed to the bank.

I arrived just after the meeting had started. After I sat down, Tom looked at me and pursed his lips in a way that meant, "So?" I winked at him in a way that meant, "Yes!" That was all we ever said about it. We spoke in code. We learned that from our dad who had learned it from Errol Flynn.

Jake: The answer is to be honest. Honesty creates sanity and sanity heals. Did you know the word "sane" could be used as a verb?

Tom: No.

Jake: Used as a verb, "sane" means "to cure, to heal." This is how I work as a psychotherapist. I help people sane themselves. We sane ourselves when we're honest. Deep, perpetual honesty fosters simplicity, ease, and intimacy in our lives. **Re**Speak makes it easier to be honest because we're not concerned about being right or wrong. We feel free to be ourselves.

Tom: You're so passionate about this.

Jake: I am.

Tom: I appreciate that. I'm also aware that honesty can hurt.

Jake: Don't you think that most of the time we hurt ourselves because we haven't been honest all along? The longer we participate in an illusion, the more we hurt ourselves when the illusion is finally revealed. The sooner we break those cycles of dysfunction by being honest, the less we hurt.

Tom: I think we're just trying to avoid feeling hurt.

Jake: I agree, but don't you think we're kidding ourselves? What would happen if we stayed honest all the time? Maybe we'd prevent the worst of hurts?

I feel like we all have a deep instinct that informs us how to live our lives so that we are "right" with ourselves. When we deviate from living this way, we cause ourselves pain and other people may cause themselves pain, which adds to our pain.

And I think that the further I get out of sync with myself, and the longer I stay disconnected from myself, the more I will suffer. So my intention is to **re**-right myself as soon as I feel "off." When I speak to Hannah in an impatient way, I try to **re**do myself, to say myself over again, as quickly as possible. Many years ago I would spend two or three days letting myself stew in my unhappiness if I treated her poorly. Today, I try to **Re**Speak myself within a minute or two.

I greatly liberate myself with the freedom to **re**view my behavior , **re**-decide how I want to behave, and then **re**do myself.

Tom: Easier said than done. You're even admitting that many years ago you weren't able to do this stuff.

Jake: Many years ago I didn't know **Re**Speak. That's what has made the biggest difference for me. Also, the way we conduct ourselves depends on whether we focus on the short term or the long term. I'll trade a little bit of discomfort today for my sanity in the longterm, which is how I think about maturity.

Tom: Maturity is sanity?

Jake: No, well, maybe that's right, but what I meant is that one aspect of maturity has to do with our perspective of time. The more mature we are, the longer our time horizon. We consider the consequences of our actions today, and what impact they will have tomorrow and beyond—even for future generations. Having a longer view of life makes it easier to tolerate the temporary discomfort that sometimes accompanies being honest.

Tom: Still, it's easier said than done.

Jake: I hear you. I also know that when we're honest about the deepest experiences we have, which are often the ones we tend to hide, we can transform ourselves. The act of revealing ourselves, such as sharing our fear of aloneness, allows us to **re**orient ourselves in relationship to our aloneness, because in the act of revealing, we are not alone. The act of revealing how much power we give to another person, power to make us feel good or feel bad, allows us to transcend our subordinate position, because we acknowledge that we are the source of the other person's power over us.

We are not subordinate to anyone. We subordinate ourselves. We are not victims, we victimize ourselves. We are not rejected, we reject ourselves; we are not criticized, we criticize ourselves. And rarely, if ever, are we deceived by another; we deceive ourselves. In my experience, self-deception is worse than being deceived by another because, if I can't rely on having an honest relationship with myself, what kind of life do I have?

Tom: A house of cards. So what's the key? How do we break our tendency to hide? Besides using ReSpeak, are there other things that make it easier to be honest?

Jake: Awareness without judgment. Stop being judgmental, or fearing other people's judgments and we become more honest.

Tom: Realistically, we have to make judgments all the time.

Jake: I agree, we make considered decisions, which are judgments, every day. What I'm talking about is when we label other people—or ourselves—in simplistic ways, as "good/bad" or "right/wrong." If we stop being judgmental in these ways we'll have an easier time being honest.

Tom: Okay, what I take from what you're saying is that we can be more aware, more curious, and not immediately form an opinion. What else can we do to be more honest?

Jake: Whatever you're doing within yourself, own yourself. Take one hundred percent responsibility for how you feel, what you think, and how you behave. People often live their lives as if they're partially responsible for themselves and partially responsible for another person, and as if the other person is partially responsible for them. This leads to dependent relationships, which tend to discourage honesty and encourage repression.

Tom: Taking one hundred percent responsibility seems radical. When we're in relationship with another person, why not take fifty percent of the responsibility?

Jake: Because the degree to which we take responsibility is the degree to which we empower ourselves. And the degree to which we don't take responsibility is the degree to which we may victimize ourselves. When we experience ourselves as victims we make excuses and blame other people. Whenever we blame other people, we aren't taking responsibility for our own experiences or our own feelings. Other people become a distraction so that we don't have to examine our contribution to creating the mess we're in.

Tom: Do you think that the only reason we blame other people is to avoid being responsible? Sometimes we blame people because they let us down or they treat us poorly.

Jake: Remember, from a **Re**ology perspective, that's not what's happening. People don't let us down or treat us poorly. They're just doing what they do. We let ourselves down with them. We disappoint ourselves with the other person's behavior. They are not doing anything to us.

Hannah and I recently went out to dinner, and we both perceived our waiter to be quite rude. I started to agitate myself and complain to Hannah about his attitude. Then I became aware of what I was doing, accepted that I was victimizing myself, and asked: "How do I want to do myself?" I didn't want to give this guy the power to ruin my evening. I didn't want to be nasty because he was nasty. That's not how I wanted to use my personal energy. I wanted to enjoy my time with Hannah. I wanted to treat the waiter in a way that made me feel good about myself. For the rest of the evening I had a clear intention about how to conduct myself, regardless of what the waiter was doing.

To me, this is a good example of the five steps of growth we talked about earlier. In a matter of just a few minutes, I became aware, accepted my feelings, asked the crucial question about how I would like to do myself, and in this case, I didn't have to await very long before I acted in a different way.

And as far as blame is concerned—particularly in our intimate relationships— the most bizarre thing we get out of blaming is connection. I can connect with you by blaming you and then fighting with you. Most of us desire connection—contact—but we don't always know the healthiest way to meet this need so we rely on whatever is familiar. For many people, conflict is the most familiar way to experience connection.

Tom: Taking one hundred percent responsibility still seems a bit extreme. I see this differently than you do. Things do happen in life. I'm not just talking about the tragedies in which people are hurt or die. There are lots of other things that happen to us. I had a friend whose wife fell out of love with him. If your wife falls out of love don't you think you would feel like someone had done something to you? Don't you think there are times when we are victims?

Jake: I certainly think that children can be victims because they're dependent on someone else to be responsible for them. If a child's caretaker is irresponsible, the child can be victimized. But with adults, for the most part I don't think of fully functioning adults as being victims.

Tom: If a woman were raped, I would say another person has victimized her. And what about being victimized by events... accidents, earthquakes, brain tumors?

Jake: I see your point and I agree that in these extreme situations, yes, we can be victims. I guess I'm saying that much of the time we're really not victims, but we victimize ourselves. Either way, the question is, as adults do we continue to victimize ourselves or do we empower ourselves? Do we get stuck in our past or live in the present? We can determine how we "do ourselves" now in relation to the past tragedy. This is the difference between children and adults; adults usually get to choose how to respond to whatever life serves up.

Tom: Not if we're dead.

Jake: True. Absolutely, but short of that, don't you think we often get warning signs? For example, people do fall out of love but not usually in a minute. This kind of thing typically happens over a period of time. There are warning signs that I can choose to pay attention to or I can ignore. If I ignore them I bear responsibility.

Tom: Just for the sake of discussion, what would you say if you found out that Hannah had done something that resulted in a terrible consequence for you?

Jake: I can imagine several responses. She's my partner and I accept that I will often impact myself with her actions. If I surprise myself by her actions, then I imagine that I've fallen asleep at the wheel and have not been paying attention to the warning signs along the way. If I really shock myself with something she does, then I would say that who Hannah is in my mind, and who she really is, are very far apart. In that case, I've been deluding myself. Although it's true that I can't ever fully know her, if we relate honestly I should be able to avoid big surprises.

Tom: So what do you say to people in situations in which we bear no responsibility—we are simply the recipients? People die, people get raped, earthquakes occur, wars break out, and we suffer the potential consequences.

Jake: I say that as long as you survive you have a choice in how you respond.

Tom: That sounds severe to me.

Jake: I don't mean to come across as severe. I'm not saying that when someone loses a leg in an earthquake, or loses someone they love, that they don't feel victimized. But what do you do with those feelings? The pain is hard enough; don't add to the pain by continuing to victimize yourself. If you hold yourself as a victim, you perpetuate your suffering. I want to eliminate suffering, but our conventional ideas about caring and compassion are often just ways of colluding with people who think of themselves as victims. This is precisely what I'm challenging.

Tom: I believe you, but you're asking a lot of people. Is it okay if I occasionally resent taking that responsibility?

Jake: What's that about? Who or what do you resent?

Tom: I don't know. People resent God or Mother Nature for the storm that kills a loved one. My friend resents his wife for falling out of love. We resent the assassins that killed Martin Luther King and John Kennedy and Bobby Kennedy.

Jake: We each make meaning in our own way when someone we love dies. We make that meaning; no one else does that for us. All I'm suggesting is that we take responsibility for the meaning we make. Your friend creates his own meaning with his wife falling out of love with him; I'm suggesting that he take responsibility for the meaning he creates. Maybe he was with the wrong partner, but he chose to be there and tolerate certain things. Maybe he needs to evaluate his own ability to be a good partner.

If you make meaning of Martin Luther King's death in a way that you cause yourself pain or sadness, take responsibility for that. Do something with your pain or sadness—use it, work with what comes to you. I inspired myself with Dr. King and turned my pain into a poem.

Tom: Really? Can you recite it?

Jake: Maybe later.

Tom: You're the one who talks about revealing yourself. Here's your chance.

Jake: Okay. I don't have a title, but this is my poem:

I have a dream of a gentle world
  Spacious and soft
A world where we each know what we value
  And we value our humanity and divinity alike
I have a dream of a world where our differences
  Don't divide us but define us
As unique and irreplaceable
  Each person standing in fullness
Oceanic in our wholeness
  I have a dream of escaping
The limited perspective of good and bad
  Right and wrong
A dream where we do not deny
  The duality of self and other
But celebrate the distinction of you and me
  For we are each alone
And in our aloneness together
  Each a light
A temporary flame
  We will extinguish
In only a moment
  So while we are here we seek to connect
To touch and be touched
  To see and be seen
To show and to say, 'This is me, I see you.'
  I have a dream today
That no one hides
  White man or black man, rich or poor
Male or female, looking or lost
  Graceful or wasteful, knowing or naught
Strong or scrawny, boastful or bashful
  For on this day we can all be free at last, free at last
Great God almighty, free at last

Tom: That's remarkable, really wonderful. I guess I shouldn't praise you, but I really like that. I didn't know there was a poet in you.

Jake: Thank you. I like the poem too. But I disappoint myself because of the ways I've held back from you. I say it right in my poem, we seek to connect, to touch and be touched, to see and be seen, but I haven't done that with you.

Tom: You're doing it now. I suppose that's what matters. According to what you've been saying, you sure as hell can't blame me. It's your responsibility.

Jake: You're such a quick study. And you're right it's my responsibility. Which brings me back to my point about being responsible without resentment. If I resent taking responsibility for myself, I'm not really accepting my responsibility.

Tom: So you think that regardless of what happens, I make my own personal meaning of it, and I should take responsibility for the meanings I make?

Jake: Who else can be responsible for the meanings that you make?

Tom: I hear you but one more example. What if you've been financially supporting me for fifteen years and one day you decide you're going to stop doing so. You've got enough money so you don't need to worry, but I've got nothing. Didn't you just do me an injustice?

Jake: I don't know, but I do know that you can negotiate with me. You're not a passive observer. You can leave me and find someone else to support you. But is that even healthy? Are you entitled to have someone support you? I don't know what you should do, but you're not without power. You're an adult and we're in an adult/adult relationship.

Tom: Or, maybe we're not. Maybe that's the problem.

Jake: True. Many people choose to stay in relationships that are not adult/adult relationships. They usually pay a price for that choice. Some people are willing to pay the price of being a victim or a martyr because they get to feel righteous, or they get to justify their anger, or they get to feel important. Although these may be ways to feel justified or powerful, that doesn't mean they're healthy.

Tom: And you want people to see that they always have choices so that they don't feel like victims.

Jake: Yes and no. Yes, I want people to see when they have choices, but I also want them to see when they don't. We don't always have the freedom to choose. We all have certain limitations, whether due to our upbringing, our lack of knowledge, our fear, or a host of other reasons. And even when we do have a choice, that doesn't mean we necessarily get to have our life any way we want it.

Tom: That's a good point. I think people often believe that the freedom to choose sounds like "I get to do what I want."

Jake: We don't always get to do what we want, but in most situations we do have options, because very few things in life are permanent and absolute. Just about everything in life is temporary, and everything is in process. We get to vote, and if we lose, we get to vote again later. We get to see our partner's behaviors, and if we don't like their behaviors we get to leave, or we get to stay and see if the behaviors change. We get to behold our own behavior, and we may not like our behavior, but we get to evolve and grow ourselves into someone we do like.

Tom: Death changes that equation. It's permanent.

Jake: It is, isn't it?

Tom: It's unlike anything else.

Jake: The finality.

Tom: Yeah.

Jake: That's why we pay so severely for withholding our love from someone who dies.

Tom: That's also true for the one who's dying.

Jake: I'm sure. And although we can do some things to clear up our relationships with people after they die, it's so much more effective to clear things up when they're living.

Tom: It's amazing. I amaze myself how I hesitate, or wait.

Jake: I amaze myself too. And every day I remind myself that short of death, nothing is permanent. If I didn't love you well before, there are consequences, but I have a chance to correct myself. If we take the time to clarify our differences and witness one another then we may be able to love each other today.

Tom: There's a lot of grace in what you're saying. I want to think about it. There's almost a paradox. On the one hand you emphasize responsibility, which includes holding ourselves accountable, but on the other hand, there's this grace—no grudges, no resentment—in the way you talk about it.

Jake: I don't see the paradox.

Tom: I know you don't. I haven't sorted it out yet. I want to think about it. I want to think about myself.

CHAPTER 14

You Are Your Own Arbiter

The previous part of our conversation had a strange quality for me because to some degree we were talking personally about the two of us, the ways we had held back, and the consequences we had experienced as a result. We were on the brink of changing that, but I heard Tom saying he hadn't decided whether or not to open up and move even closer. We were flirting with intimacy in ways that were new to both of us. I didn't know where this would lead.

As our conversation continued I was curious to see what Tom would do.

Jake: Where did we leave off?

Tom: Here's my overriding concern about all that we've discussed. You talk about wanting to provide a way for people to empower themselves and to feel more relaxed in their lives. But then you go on and suggest that the world is, as you describe it, arbitrary. That doesn't help me relax.

Jake: I'm not exactly saying that "the world" is arbitrary, but that the way we make meaning of the world is arbitrary. There are physical laws, such as gravity, that are not arbitrary. There are many things that are not arbitrary. But the way we make meaning is arbitrary—the meaning we assign to things varies.

Look at the two of us; we're a perfect example. In the last several weeks we've changed the way we relate. The context of our lives changed, our relationship took on new meaning. We changed. Although the idea that meaning is arbitrary may be frightening, I also find this to be tremendously liberating.

Tom: I see that.

Jake: This is how we renew ourselves. You determine what's meaningful to you. If you then live in accordance with what's meaningful to you, you've set a direction for your life; you've got your own personal compass. Pursuing what you think is meaningful, with some measure of realism, is a privilege—one that not everybody has.

Tom: If we each make meaning for ourselves, then why do you say it's a privilege that not everyone has?

Jake: Some people live in a context where all they can think about or pursue is survival. Those of us who don't have to worry about survival on a daily basis are the ones who have the privilege of choosing how to live our lives.

Tom: And what did you mean by "some measure of realism"? I don't think I've heard you talk about that before.

Jake: I'm talking about being practical. If I want to be a pilot I need to take flying lessons. If I want to have an intimate relationship I need to develop the relevant skills. If I want to be a leader I need to learn how to lead.

I don't believe that positive thinking alone will always create the results we want in our lives. There are times—many times—when we have to put in effort, pay our dues, so to speak.

Tom: You enliven yourself with this idea that meaning is arbitrary, don't you?

Jake: I do now. When I first awoke to the idea I felt very uneasy and depressed myself for quite a while, probably a couple of years. I contemplated nihilism—the idea that nothing matters. I considered existentialism—the idea that individuals must struggle to exist in a universe that has no meaning. I depressed myself with these ideas, but like many people, I missed the important point.

Tom: Which point?

Jake: The point isn't that there's no meaning. The point is that meaning is arbitrary; and each of us is our own arbiter. We continually create meaning; we can't not create meaning. The world that I'm responding to in each moment is the world in my own mind. Everyone creates their own world—makes their own meaning; they just may not know that they're doing so. Why not create your world so that you **re**new yourself and can pursue your passions?

Tom: What you're saying implies that even the meaning of death is something we create for ourselves.

Jake: Especially death. Because who knows exactly what death means? Any meaning we impose upon death has to be made up. My own belief is that if we live a rich and meaningful life, we're more likely to experience a gentle and meaningful death.

Tom: I'm still uncertain.

Jake: That's why I depressed myself for a couple of years. I had a hard time accepting all this uncertainty.

Tom: What helped you come out of your depression?

Jake: I looked at everything I knew about human nature. I investigated the lives of people who suffer and other people who were unusually productive, healthy, and happy. I boiled it down to four things. The first was to address our core pattern. Second was to individuate from our parents. Third was to live according to our values. And fourth was to learn to use language in a new way—and that turned out to be **Re**Speak.

Tom: I'd like to hear you talk more about each of those, but first I have a question. What if you had a year to live? What would you focus on?

Jake: I don't know, Tommy. I think I'd just go to an island with Hannah and not worry about any of this stuff.

Tom: But isn't that partially because you've spent your entire life doing this stuff? I imagine you feel somewhat complete.

Jake: I'm not sure about feeling complete, but I feel like I'm awake and consciously choosing the way I live.

CHAPTER 15

You Can Go To Your Core or Keep Chasing Your Tales

Tom and I went scuba diving for the first time when I was in my late teens and he was in his twenties. This guy—Leroy—took us out in a small boat. He had a scar across his entire belly that got my attention. His only instructions were to follow him and do whatever he told us to do.

At one point, when we were at least sixty feet deep, Leroy signaled us to stay in that exact spot and then he disappeared. I guess he went up to see where we were. I don't really know what he did, but Tom and I hovered in place waiting for him to return, which he did.

Our parents refer to that day as the time when the two of us were the most excited they'd ever seen us. We came back to shore after our adventure and couldn't stop talking about it. Our scuba diving experience remained one of our great stories, a tale of two brothers.

Tom: I intrigue myself with your comment about going away to an island with Hannah. Would that be a responsible thing to do?

Jake: Absolutely. Because, for me, being responsible isn't limited to making sacrifices or assuming burdens. Being responsible means taking responsibility for my personal conduct—how I behave, treat other people, express myself, and care for myself.

When we conduct ourselves well, we feel good about ourselves, our self-talk becomes more positive, our self-esteem improves. And then, because we're comfortable within ourselves, we expend less energy trying to convince other people that we're okay. As we take this level of responsibility for ourselves, we gain some sense of control in our lives.

Assuming responsibility—as I describe it—isn't a burden, it's freeing. Have you ever heard of the newspaper test?

Tom: No.

Jake: The idea is to imagine that whatever you do today will be on the front page of the newspaper tomorrow. If you expect that will happen, you're more likely to conduct yourself in a way that you'll feel good about, a responsible way. I'd feel great about myself if I spent the last year of my life on an island with Hannah, assuming I treated her really well.

Tom: So why do you think that some people conduct themselves in ways they don't feel good about? Ways you would call irresponsible.

Jake: Great question.

Tom: Give me a great answer.

Jake: I think I can. Although there can be a few reasons why we behave irresponsibly, the most common reason is that we tolerate our own immaturity.

Tom: Ouch! And how do we change this?

Jake: Okay, so a few minutes ago I mentioned four things we can do—all of them help us become more responsible and more mature. Again, we need to address our limiting core patterns, individuate, discover what we really value, and learn **ReSpeak**.

Let's start by talking about our core patterns. When we address our limiting core patterns we take a big step in maturing ourselves. We can either go to our core—taking responsibility for these patterns—or we can spend our lives chasing our tales, t-a-l-e-s, the stories we tell ourselves to justify our behaviors.

When I talk about our limiting core patterns, I'm referring to immature beliefs and behaviors we rely on to minimize our anxiety and avoid discomfort—emotional discomfort. These are defense mechanisms that help us feel safe. We may have served ourselves well with these patterns when we first developed them, but by the time we're adults, we hamper ourselves by repeating the same patterns.

Our core patterns are outdated ways of coping. As long as we rely on these patterns, we remain hostage to our pasts. If we learn to see our core patterns—and take responsibility for them —we can heal our relationship with our pasts and grow ourselves up, **re**new ourselves.

Working with our core patterns is so much more powerful than addressing our problems at the surface level—chasing all of our symptoms and trying to eradicate them one at a time. When we work at these deeper levels, the progress can be profound, but working at these deep levels requires a gentle touch.

Tom: Why a gentle touch?

Jake: So that we don't arouse our defenses. The safer we feel, the deeper we can go, and these patterns are pretty deep. I've identified only four of these limiting core patterns. We confuse ourselves. We overwhelm ourselves. We conflict ourselves. Or we depress ourselves. These are the origins of our emotional struggles.

Tom: I do three of the four.

Jake: I suppose we all do a few of these to varying degrees, but usually one of these will be our core pattern. Notice how you're responding to your illness. That'll give you a clue. Whenever we're under a lot of stress we're likely to default to our core pattern. Do you overwhelm yourself, conflict yourself, or depress yourself?

Tom: Depress myself.

Jake: So let's talk about that, but first I want to explain how these patterns develop, okay?

Tom: Go ahead. I suspect I'll still be depressed by time we get to my pattern.

Jake: Maybe not. Wouldn't that be thrilling? Most of these core patterns develop between the time of our birth and the time we're about six or seven. These first six or seven years of life—which I call the infancy stage—are typically less than ten percent of our entire life, but this stage has a disproportionately large impact on our development.

During our first couple of years of life, we need to establish a separate sense of our physical selves. If we don't succeed at this, our core pattern becomes severe confusion. I'm not talking about regular confusion, but rather the kind of confusion in which we don't know where we begin and end, or where other people begin and end.

This sort of confusion can contribute to psychosis or other forms of serious mental illness later in life. People who seek help for this kind of problem later in life usually end up being medicated or finding some kind of pacification therapy. To become an independently functioning adult we need to accomplish this basic separation early in life.

Tom: If we don't, can we go back and fix this?

Jake: It's very hard. If you started this process of separation, but never quite completed it, there is some hope of completing it later in life, but it's tough.

Tom: So, if early in life I don't experience myself as being physically separate, I'm in trouble? You're saying our core pattern of confusion will be really debilitating.

Jake: That's right, but if we do sense our physical self as separate, then we naturally move to the next stage of development. Between ages two to four, we need to develop a sense of our separate emotional selves. If we don't, later in life we'll struggle with the core pattern of overwhelming ourselves. This pattern stems from our relationship with our primary caregiver, usually our mother. It's crucial to experience our emotions as ours, and to recognize our mother's emotions as hers, not ours. Creating these distinctions is the foundation that allows us to form healthy emotional boundaries. When we have healthy emotional boundaries we avoid co-dependent relationships because we know how to care for ourselves, comfort ourselves and attend to our emotional needs.

Tom: Can you say more about attending to our emotional needs?

Jake: Your emotions are an expression of your nervous system. You always have access to your own nervous system, which means you can influence yourself and work with yourself— attend to yourself. You can do things to calm and comfort yourself. But how can you work with emotions you experience if they belong to someone else? If you try to calm me down so that you'll feel better, that means you're trying to influence my nervous system to make yourself feel better.

Tom: We all do that at times. If someone's sad, we try to cheer them up, if someone's angry we try to calm them down. It is possible to influence another person's nervous system.

Jake: But *how* we do it is the key. When I use **Re**Speak, I tell you how I'm experiencing myself in relationship to you, but I won't try to change you to make myself feel better. Too often we try to influence other people in ways that result in us taking responsibility for them. Although we may be able to influence

141

their nervous systems, it's risky business, and if it's not done very consciously it fosters co-dependency and confusion about our emotional boundaries.

Tom: How does this relate to the core pattern of feeling overwhelmed?

Jake: If you don't create clear emotional boundaries, you can easily end up feeling overwhelmed because you can't sort out whose emotions belong to whom. You may feel as if other people's emotions are yours or, at least, you burden yourself with their emotions. There's also a tendency to feel as if everything is about you. As a result, you become overly sensitive, or you become emotionally illiterate—oblivious—as a way to cope with feeling overwhelmed. This leads to self-centeredness and narcissism.

Tom: I'm not sure I understand the distinction between being overwhelmed and being confused. They seem very similar to me.

Jake: People who suffer from the kind of confusion I was talking about are not really able to manage their lives. People who overwhelm themselves may feel burdened to the point of confusion, but they do have a fundamental sense of self and they are able to manage their lives.

Tom: If my core pattern is that I overwhelm myself, I don't imagine I can do much to help myself when I'm an infant. So what do I do when I'm fifty-six years old and I realize this is my core pattern?

Jake: You're right, we can't do anything about this when we're infants. We probably can't even take full responsibility for this pattern when we're in our teens. But once we're in our twenties or thirties, and for the rest of our adult lives, it's possible to take responsibility for these patterns of behavior that we learned during our earliest years. To me, this is part of growing up—maturing. What else are we going to do? How long can we blame our parents? How long can we victimize ourselves with our history? And that's what we'll be doing if we continue to rely on outdated, immature ways of behaving.

Tom: So what do we do?

Jake: For one thing, we come to realize and accept that we won't always get all of our needs met. This is part of how we break the cycle of narcissism: we realize that people have competing needs and we don't always get exactly what we want. If we're fortunate, we learn this when we're very young, before the age of four. We discover that we can survive our emotional disappointments. An interesting part of parenting is accepting that you're going to disappoint your infant sooner or later. We tend to be afraid of this, but it's not entirely a bad thing. Of course, it depends how often it happens and how serious the situation is, but some mild disappointment in which your child learns to take care of himself can contribute to his overall sense of well-being.

Another thing we need to do is internalize the role of caretaker by learning how to comfort and soothe ourselves, not just create distractions, when there is no one around to care for us. This frees us from our emotional dependence on others.

Finally, we must be able to establish appropriate boundaries. This means not asking other people to assume responsibility for us. It means not assuming responsibility for others. It means managing the contexts of our lives so that we don't put ourselves in certain situations that we know we can't handle.

Tom: It's interesting to me that you said we probably can't do this during our teenaged years, because both Clarissa and Rand are teenagers and it's so obvious to me how helpful it would be to learn this at that young age.

Jake: It would be great and it's worth trying. My only caution is that teens tend to be so concerned about how they're perceived by their peers that they strongly react to other people's nervous systems.

Tom: It still seems like it would be helpful. I can see how using ReSpeak would help people—even teenagers—feel less overwhelmed because they don't feel as if the world is doing something to them. Just changing my language from "I am overwhelmed," to "I overwhelm myself" changes my relationship, my boundary, with the world.

Jake: I agree. I think **ReSpeak** is the ultimate way to redefine our boundaries; it's as if we **re**draw our emotional maps.

Tom: That's a nice way to say it. I can actually feel that.

Jake: I don't often hear you talk about how you feel. Is that new for you or just something we never talk about?

Tom: I think it's both, but I'm certainly more aware of my feelings than I used to be. Sometimes I'm not clear about how I feel, I'm conflicted, and I like to be clear before I talk about things.

Jake: You may be particularly interested in the third core pattern. This is the pattern of conflicting ourselves. This pattern is the result of not creating a separate mental identity of ourselves around the age of four through six. No one develops a full Identity so early in life. It's not realistic to do so. But some of us cut off and disown big parts of ourselves because we're told that these parts are unacceptable, and this leads to inner conflict.

Around the age of four the language center revs up in our brains. With our newfound language skills we begin to repress the things we find intolerable. Language that makes this possible—with language we can dissociate or cut off aspects of ourselves. I remember learning this. If I behaved poorly, Mom would say to me, "You can send your 'bad boy' to the attic to play with your train set, and when you decide to be a 'good boy' you can come back down and be with me." What a powerful lesson in dissociating: send the "bad" part of yourself away and when you find the "good" part, come back to be with me.

My point is that around the age of four, we start using language to repress and disconnect from parts of ourselves. The degree to which we disconnect or cut off parts of ourselves is the degree to which we don't accept ourselves. And this self-alienation causes internal conflicts that show up later in life.

Tom: I'm not clear why the self-alienation leads to conflict.

Jake: Because the parts of ourselves that we've rejected, disowned, and banished don't truly disappear—they continue to want what they want. The parts we cut off don't die; they're dormant, they lie in hiding, waiting for a time when they can reemerge. And while they're hiding, they're influencing us because they are us. Until we accept and integrate our hidden beliefs, our unmet needs, our shames, our regrets and our fears about who we are, they will sabotage us—we will sabotage ourselves.

Along the way, we will exhaust ourselves because hiding consumes a lot of energy. Some parts of us want one thing, other parts want something else. We repress the parts we don't like, but we know that they are in us. No matter how much love we receive from other people, we won't feel satiated because we're saying, "If you only knew." But the people trying to love us don't know, so we live in fear that they'll find out. As a result, intimacy remains elusive.

Tom: But it's normal to have parts of us that want one thing, say, to be promiscuous, while other parts want something else, say, to be monogamous.

Jake: And as adults we sort out our internal conflicts. We rely on our reason and intuition to make choices and decisions. We then take responsibility for our decisions. At least we do if we're mature.

Tom: But we can't do that when we're five years old.

Jake: Exactly. So we end up feeling embarrassed, ashamed, resentful, etcetera by our own behaviors, which we then try to forget or hide.

Tom: And what are you suggesting we do about this?

Jake: You can **re**discover the aspects of yourself that you've been hiding. You can come to understand why you cut off or disowned certain parts of yourself. You can begin to see that some of your behaviors today are ways you compensate for the parts of yourself that you have hidden. With awareness and acceptance you can start to integrate these parts of yourself. The solution is acceptance and integration.

Tom: What if you really hate some part of yourself to the point where accepting it is totally unrealistic?

Jake: That makes this very hard. To move beyond such judgments requires letting go of the harsh ways we talk about and to ourselves. As we soften our language we're more likely to develop understanding and compassion. Some clients I work with can't find their own compassion so I offer them mine.

Tom: I imagine that if someone starts with this kind of intense judgment, the process of change takes a long time.

Jake: Yes and no. In one sense, growing up—which is what we're talking about—takes a lifetime. It's a life-long journey. However, there are certain steps along the way that can be instantly transformative. There are times in life when we see what needs to be done, the need is compelling, and we do it. We promise to stop doing something or to start doing something, and we don't back away from our commitment.

What's so troubling to me is—as I said before—the degree to which many people tolerate their own immaturity. We know what we need to do, but we reserve the right to behave in childish ways. We continue to indulge in tantrums, moodiness, self-absorption, addictive behaviors, and self-pity, all of which muddy up our emotional footprint.

Tom: Are those behaviors signs that a person is conflicted?

Jake: They're signs of immaturity. They can be the result of any of the limiting core patterns.

Tom: Speaking of which, we never talked about my tendency to depress myself.

Jake: The pattern of depressing ourselves comes from having not developed healthy beliefs or scripts during our "young childhood" years, which are ages seven to twenty. If we don't develop healthy beliefs, we're less likely to develop healthy self-esteem. We need generative ideas about the world and about ourselves that allow us to feel good about who we are, and feel hopeful about our futures. Without healthy beliefs, ones that promote hope, we're apt to depress ourselves.

During young childhood, we're becoming a bit less dependent. As we begin to venture out into the world we use our beliefs to guide us. Typically, we start with beliefs that we learned from our parents, and then we begin to edit these beliefs and make them our own.

Do our beliefs foster optimism? Or do they foster fear? Do we believe we're capable of dealing with the challenges that come our way? Or do we believe we will never get what we want? Do we believe we should take as much as we can? Or do we believe we should give as much as we can? Do we believe life is fair? Or do we believe it's unfair?

Our beliefs, which we will continue to modify for years to come, shape the ways we see the world. They influence every aspect of our lives, including our patterns of attraction—meaning the people we attract into our lives.

Tom: It seems to me that if we don't develop healthy beliefs when we're young, it's hard to develop them later in life because we have years of evidence to support our unhealthy beliefs.

Jake: I agree with you. If we develop negative beliefs about ourselves and then spend years validating those beliefs, we create a hurdle for ourselves. At some point, we may choose to **re**examine our beliefs and **re**educate ourselves. If we want to dismantle outdated beliefs, we'll need to find counter-examples to disprove our old beliefs. We'll also need to create new experiences that support our new beliefs. This is a process of **re**educating and **re**defining ourselves. It's exactly what people do when they come to our **re**treats.

Tom: I assume the people who go to your retreats have different core patterns. So do they each focus on different things?

Jake: They all learn a new way to speak to themselves and other people. And then they do individual work that varies depending on their issues and their core patterns. Let's say a woman overwhelms herself; her focus will be on learning to develop appropriate emotional boundaries. Whereas a man who conflicts himself—that's his core pattern—he'll focus on developing greater self-acceptance. And for people who tend to depress themselves, they focus on **re**evaluating and **re**creating their belief systems.

The one thing that's consistent, regardless of your limiting core pattern, is that you are the only one who can take responsibility for your pattern. As soon as you do so, you shift into an adult relationship with your self.

Tom: Why do you put so much emphasis on the core patterns?

Jake: Because once I understood my core pattern I didn't have to stop and dissect every difficult interaction in my life. I just focused on the one basic theme, which for me is overwhelming myself. I also conflict myself a bit, but mostly I overwhelm myself.

I realize that if I take the time to create very clear boundaries, and if I take the time to attend to my own emotions, I'm able to conduct myself in ways that I feel good about. I pass the newspaper test.

Once I knew my core pattern, I **re**cognized that I wasn't going to get all of my emotional needs met by someone else. I understood that some of my needs were childish. I was able to take responsibility for my pattern by saying to Hannah, "I wish you could read my mind and take care of all my needs. I wish you could protect me from things I'm scared of. I wish you could always make me feel good about myself." Then I would add, "And I know that you can't do these things for me. I need to do them for myself."

When I revealed myself in this way, giving a mature voice to some of my childhood feelings, I raised the level of our conversation to an adult/adult conversation. I stopped denying my childhood feelings and then I stopped unconsciously acting out these parts of myself. I took responsibility for myself by creating clear boundaries—clarifying what I expected of myself and what I expected of Hannah—and I calmed down because these parts of me were witnessed instead of being hidden away.

So, I did two things. I created clear boundaries and I accepted some aspects of myself that I previously had denied.

Tom: This is really interesting to me. I do a couple of the patterns too, but I see now so clearly that my primary pattern is depressing myself. Does that surprise you?

Jake: Not really. I've heard you say things such as, "Life isn't fair," or "People don't get what they deserve." If these are representative of your belief system, I can see why you might depress yourself.

Tom: Unfortunately, I have a lot of evidence to support those beliefs. We know plenty of really good people who haven't gotten what they deserve in life. Mom and Dad are the prime example. What's happening to me doesn't feel terribly fair. So I defend my depression.

There's one thing I don't understand about these core patterns. You believe that we have an innate desire to grow, yet we hinder our growth with these core patterns. That seems like a contradiction.

Jake: When we created our core patterns early in life, they actually supported our growth. Those patterns were the only way we knew to minimize our anxiety, to cope. That was their purpose. But they're children's tools. When we get to be adults, these tools no longer serve us.

Imagine a rubber band being stretched. One end is being pulled by our childlike desire to be taken care of, to please and be pleased, to avoid conflict. The other end is pulling us toward the individuality, autonomy, and the responsibility of adulthood. The longer we hold on, the more tension we experience in our lives, because we are adults living as children.

Tom: I can imagine the terrible sting we feel if we let go of one end.

Jake: That's the sting of individuating.

CHAPTER 16

Individuating

The next part of our conversation took place when Tom was in the hospital. I unnerved myself seeing my older brother lying in a hospital bed. I don't like being in hospitals. I tend to shut down, but I knew that wasn't helpful in this situation so I tried to be present for those who were there. I wanted to be a comfort to my brother and his family, but I felt raw and struggled just to comfort myself. Tommy seemed so helpless. I didn't know what to do for him. In my entire life we'd never been affectionate. I watched my sister stroking his head, massaging his neck, putting blankets on him when he was cold, taking them off two minutes later when he was hot. I watched Vicky feeding him and giving him ice chips to soothe him. I wished I were equally comfortable nurturing him. I simply held his hand.

I tried to find time with him when we could be alone; I felt more comfortable when it was just the two of us. During my second visit, he was more alert. He opened his eyes and looked at me without expression. There was no affect. None. Just his beautiful blue eyes. I asked him several questions about how he was feeling, but he clearly didn't want to talk about himself or his situation.

He seemed pleased to tell me which stores I should go to so that I could buy some warmer clothes. Tom loved to shop. He always knew the best stores, as well as the places to go to get a bargain.

Eventually he said, "Keep telling me about your book, I find it helpful—I help myself." I hesitated to talk about anything.

Continuing our conversation seemed disconnected from the hospital reality, but I realized that's just because of the way I constructed the hospital reality in my mind. I didn't have to make myself glum and morose.

When I did start talking with Tom—picking up where we left off —I perceived he was not only interested, but he seemed to relax.

Jake: We were talking about individuating, which is a process that helps us grow up and become healthy, autonomous adults. I think it should be honored with some kind of ritual, but unfortunately it's not practiced as a ritual in most parts of our culture. To individuate we need to disidentify with our parents. This is our major developmental task during what I call the "old child" stage of development, which extends from about age 20-35.

Tom: Still a child at 35?

Jake: The developmental model that John Weir developed—and I've continued to refine—suggests that we're "young children" from 7-20, "old children" from 20-35, then "young adults" from 35-50, "old adults" from 50-65, then "elders" from 65-80, and "actualized" after 80. It's an unusual way to look at people, but quite profound and it can be extremely helpful.

Until we disidentify with our parents and learn to identify ourselves as adults in the world, we don't fully live the lives of adults. Before we fully individuate, to varying degrees, we live the emotional life of a child, which means either we're dependent or we're rebellious—emotionally.

To individuate requires that we face our childhood fears, take responsibility for ourselves, and choose to live courageously. This includes recognizing the voices of 'Mom' and 'Dad' that we internalized as children and saying goodbye to them…I'm having a hard time talking with you about this.

Tom: Why?

Jake: It's the idea of saying "goodbye" to Mom and Dad. That's supposed to be a metaphor, not literal, but it seems surreal here in this situation.

Tom: Well, you can't stop now. And if it helps, I find this comforting. The more we talk, the better I feel about myself. So keep going.

Jake: Okay. Most people are still working on this well into their forties and fifties, even sixties. It's more constructive to individuate when our parents are alive, but we can work on this even after they've died. How old we are when we individuate isn't what matters. What matters, as adults, is that we individuate—the sooner the better.

Tom: How old were you?

Jake: Remember when I was sixteen and I left home? That was an unconscious attempt to individuate. But it was premature for me. My next attempt was when I was twenty-six; I took my first conscious steps to individuate. At the time I was living in Vermont and Mom and Dad were living in Connecticut. I drove to see them one weekend intending to let them know I wanted to change the nature of our relationship. I wanted to start communicating with them in an adult/adult manner. The challenge for me was that their approval and recognition of me was still a significant source of sustenance in my life.

I don't remember all the details, but I tried to have a conversation with them. I was standing at the foot of their bed. I explained to them that I was trying to take more responsibility for myself and they seemed very supportive. Then I shared with them how hard it was for me to be out in the world, alone. Not long after that I was sitting on the end of their bed crying, and they were comforting me. That night I slept in my old bedroom. I spent the weekend allowing them to comfort me. Sunday afternoon I headed back to Vermont, somewhat embarrassed, knowing that I hadn't succeeded in my task to show them that

I'd individuated. And that was part of the problem; I was doing it to show them, not doing it just for me.

Two or three years later I tried again. I attempted to have an adult/adult conversation with them, but I was kind of harsh in my delivery, kind of cold. They both seemed slightly put off and yet I didn't know any other way. I behaved more like a rebellious adolescent than an adult and I knew that, once again, I hadn't accomplished my purpose.

My life continued. My first marriage came to an end, and I planned to leave Vermont and move to New Mexico. I knew I wanted to have "the conversation" with Mom and Dad before I left, so I tried again. I drove to their home, but I let them know that I wouldn't be staying with them. I was just going to have a short visit and I'd be sleeping at a nearby motel. The evening I arrived I spent time talking with Mom. We had what felt like a genuine adult/adult conversation. I wasn't invested in her response, but I was interested in her perspective. I was also interested to learn more about her as a person. I felt calm and mature.

It was strange to go to a hotel that night, but very helpful. The next morning, after breakfast, I took a long walk with Dad. We also had an adult/adult conversation, the first of many. He shared things with me. He talked about wishing he'd made some different choices in his life, mostly around his work. I felt very appreciative of him and proud of myself.

I was better able to appreciate both of them as I stepped away from them. They had made some mistakes with me when I was a kid, but they had given me one of the most valuable things a kid can have, the belief that I'm lovable.

My process of individuating has continued since then, but it was during that last visit that I completed my ritual. My role as an adult feels very natural to me. As I've moved into the prime of my life, Mom and Dad have begun their decline. I frequently remind myself that I'm no longer a child, even though at times, I long to be cared for as if I were a child. Seeing Dad after he broke his hip, helpless in a hospital bed, was another step in my journey. Accepting Mom's account of her history with me, even though I see our history differently, was another step in my journey. I no longer look to them for approval and I no longer react to them with disapproval. They live their lives. I live mine. The next step in my journey of individuating will be to individuate more than I already have from Hannah. And that process is well under way.

Tom: How do you think you know if you've individuated?

Jake: Ask yourself: Who determines my self-esteem? Is it based on what my parents think of me, or my partner, or my peers, or does my esteem come primarily from within me? Do I live my life according to the values I learned as a child, or have I discovered my own values? When I'm in the presence of my parents, my partner, or others, can I be completely and fully myself, or do I unnecessarily edit myself? When I go home for the holidays, do I feel like the person I've become or the person every one remembers from childhood?

How we respond to our partners reveals how far along we are in the process of individuating. Disidentifying from our parents is the first step towards individuating, but the process goes beyond that. Most of us use our first truly serious romantic relationship as a vehicle to help us further individuate. We transfer many of our needs from our parents to our partners.

Some needs, which our parents fulfilled—like taking responsibility for us—our partners shouldn't fulfill, and we have to deal with our feelings about that. Some needs that our parents couldn't satisfy, such as our sexual needs, our partners can satisfy. Even though our partnership is considered an adult/ adult relationship, many of us are still quite dependent, often relating in a child/child or child/adult dynamic. Hopefully, we use our partnership or our marriages to become more independent and learn how to relate in an adult/adult way.

Once we're in a partnership we can ask: Have I transferred my need for approval from my parents to my partner? Do I project my childish needs onto my partner? Do I over-react to my partner? How much power do I give to my partner? How dependent am I on my partner for my sense of self—for my emotional well-being? Am I too dependent on my partner to soothe and reassure me?

Honestly answering these questions can help you see where you are in your process of individuating. Are you still trying to disidentify with your parents? Are you using your partner to do so? Unless you're overt about this, relating with your partner can be very confusing. If you're clear and honest, you increase your chances for success.

Tom: And to you, what does success look like?

Jake: You learn to live together as two independent people who care deeply for each other. You rely on each other in certain ways without being dependent on each other. I like the expression that "two healthy me's create a healthy we." This can take time to accomplish.

Tom: Can success be that you find someone that completely satisfies your emotional needs?

Jake: I don't think that's realistic. That idea is a remnant from childhood. No one is going to satisfy all your emotional needs on an ongoing basis. Eventually, you'll disappoint yourself. If your partner gives too much, you'll become dependent. If she doesn't give enough, you'll frustrate yourself.

Tom: So we have to learn to satisfy ourselves.

Jake: Actually, I don't think that's realistic either. I mean, yes, we need to learn to satisfy ourselves, but we don't do that entirely independent of other people. We need people. We need to be loved. We need to be appreciated. And we need to assess if our needs are appropriate. Do we need too much from another person? Do we need more than we are willing to admit?

These are the struggles we go through to achieve independence. If we succeed, then we become stronger as individuals and stronger as a couple. If we fail, we'll either remain in a marriage of mediocrity, we'll continue to fight, or we'll go our separate ways.

Using our partner as a means to disidentify with our parents isn't a bad thing. I see this as natural and appropriate. My main point is that if we're consciously aware that this is occurring, the process is much easier.

Based on my experience as a therapist, I think that most adults remain their parents' children forever. I don't mean this literally, because in that sense we're always our parents' children. I'm talking about our beliefs and internal Identity. I think that when most people die, they're still living a role in which they feel like their parents' child. Most people do not find a way to fully grow themselves up and take complete responsibility for their lives.

Tom: Why's it so difficult?

Jake: In part, because we don't even talk about it. Most parents have no training related to these concepts. Most kids are left on their own to figure themselves out. And if we don't understand the need to individuate, and the process to individuate, we waste so much personal energy trying to maintain illusions, trying to control people, trying to get others to take care of us or us taking care of them.

I'll tell you a short story about a very bright, highly educated woman I recently worked with. She came to see me because she was having a hard time with her husband. Either she would crumble when he was mad, or she would escalate and become madder and meaner than she perceived him to be. She was exhausting herself.

I asked her why she didn't have an adult/adult conversation with him and she said, "He reminds me of my mother." She went on, "I remember when my mother would treat me poorly, like the time she told me I was dumb. I got upset and started to cry. I told my mother that she upset me. She got angry and said, 'You always do that—you always blame me. I can't do anything without being misunderstood.'"

Then my client said, "I couldn't believe she made me out to be wrong when she was the one who had told me I was dumb. All I wanted was her attention, and the only way I could get her attention was to be wrong, to take the blame, even when I didn't do anything. My dad couldn't live with her being upset, so he always told me to apologize to Mom. There was another time when my mother said, 'I had a daughter once, but you're not my daughter any more.'"

My client said, "I was furious, but because my mother was upset, my father told me to apologize."

I asked my client, "When did this happen?" and she told me it had been over fifteen years ago. She had been carrying this around and continuing to relive these scenes and conversations. I said to her, "It's time for you to stop wasting your energy fighting old battles. You're no longer your mother's little girl. You're a grown woman. Your mother is no longer responsible for your well being, you are." She asked, "How do I do that?" I explained she could start by using **Re**Speak because it's an adult language. She asked me to give her an example of how she could express herself.

I spoke as if I were her, demonstrating how she could use **Re**Speak to talk about her mother. I placed extra emphasis on the pronoun "I." "*I* choose to engage with my mother. In doing so, *I* choose not to get my emotional needs met. *I* tolerate what

I see as her narcissism. *I* agree to play this crazy-making game, acting as though everything is about her. *I* deprive myself when she isn't available for me. *I* sacrifice my integrity so *I* can have her in my life.

"*I* even fool myself with my father because I perceive him as doing nothing more than colluding with my mother. I perceive him as narcissistic in his own way, asking me to sacrifice myself so that he can have peace in his life. I experience him as extremely selfish, yet *I* choose to engage with him. *I* choose to engage with people who can't give me what I want. *I* put up with my mother when she says things like, 'I had a daughter once, but you're not my daughter.'

"*I* disrespect myself with this woman and go back for more. Why? Because *I* don't want to accept that I'll never get what I want from her. If I could accept that, maybe I could let go and stop beating my head against the wall. If I had better self-esteem I would simply refuse to relate with people who I perceive as crazy. If I stopped relating with such people, I'd have better self-esteem.

"Being with my husband is a chance for me to conduct myself in a totally different way. When he's not emotionally available, for the most part, we can talk it through. Although *I* did pick a man who on occasion *I* use to threaten myself just the way I threatened myself with my mother, *I* can break this pattern by conducting myself in a different way, even when I scare myself. This means that from now on I won't withdraw and I won't get angry, because those are outdated ways of behaving that I used with my mother. They didn't work then. They won't work now. *I* amaze myself that *I* haunt myself with this woman whom I perceive as crazy and selfish. I need to say goodbye to her."

My client was weeping when I finished. She told me, "I'm crying because I can't believe that I've done THAT to myself! And kept on doing it all these years! And yet, even realizing that yes I did do that, and have, and still do—the idea of not engaging with my parents and having a meaningful connection, seems very very difficult."

That's the story of a very smart person who hadn't individuated. Since she never created appropriate emotional boundaries, she held herself hostage with other people's nervous systems. She felt overwhelmed much of the time and in response, she either caved in or got angry. Neither of these responses helped her get what she wanted, which was loving contact. In her husband she found someone who helped her justify these outdated ways of behaving, and she partially remained an emotional child. This is what happens if we don't individuate—we end up living an exhausting, crazy-making life.

Tom: What happened to your client?

Jake: A few months later she told me, "I've been struggling with the idea of not engaging with my mother and it's very hard because I think of myself as a loving person. But with your help, I've realized this isn't about my mother, it's about me. Focusing on her is a waste of my energy. I've decided to stop trying to express my love to my mother, and instead, express my love to my husband, but not engage with him when things are dysfunctional. I'm no longer going to play into those patterns of behavior, not with him, not with her, and not in myself. I feel like this gives me a place to stand that feels strong and balanced and loving, while refusing to perpetuate the pattern of dysfunction and dependence."

Tom: She sounds like a different woman. I wonder if part of her problem was that she didn't know what she wanted. Did she want her mother's approval and love or did she want to let go of her past and create something different with her husband?

Jake: I think that's a big part of what happened. The child within wanted her mother's love. She didn't want to give up the possibility of getting that. But ultimately, she accepted that she would have to live with a hole that could never be filled.

Tom: Never?

Jake: Never. Some of our early needs can only be satiated when we're really young. If we don't get those crucial needs met, we need to live with the hole inside of us.

Tom: And then we're what? Flawed, broken, limited?

Jake: Human.

Tom: Maybe you're right, the client you just talked about doesn't sound flawed.

Jake: She's become a beautiful woman and a great partner for her husband. She learned what it is that she truly values as an adult. And she gave up the old fight.

Tom: I value sleep. Can we continue tomorrow?

Jake: I'll be here.

CHAPTER 17

Renew Yourself By Living
According To What You Value

When I visited with Tom the next day he seemed even more energetic and alert. I surprised myself, and realized that I was expecting him to get worse. This seemed to be how I was preparing myself for what appeared to be inevitable. I troubled myself with my "preparing for the worst." I wanted to hold a completely positive attitude because I appreciated the power of thought. But I was also trying to be honest with myself about the seriousness of the situation.

How do you acknowledge a tragedy while still allowing for a miracle?

I found a rhythm that ebbed and flowed. Sometimes I was very present and calm. Other times I frightened and upset myself. I would reach my limit, then leap to hope or denial.

I amazed myself with how my expectations adapted: when this crises had begun I had been horrified by the idea that Tommy might only live a couple of years, but just a few weeks later I found myself desperately hoping he would live for six more months. I heard myself bargaining in my own mind, "Just give him six months of being conscious and able to direct the final stage of his life. Give him the time he needs to do what he wants to do, and say what he wants to say to his family and friends." But what did I have to bargain with? And with whom was I making this deal?

Tom: Where'd we leave off?

Jake: We spent some time talking about addressing our core patterns, and yesterday, I shared a story about my client individuating, and you said it sounded like her values changed. That's exactly right, and this brings us to the third thing in my list of four that we can do to promote our growth and learn healthier ways of relating—discover what we really value.

Our values evolve as our Identity evolves. Individuating is a prerequisite to discovering our own values. But, even after we individuate, our values continue to evolve and change. We can help ourselves by pausing every so often and asking: "What do I value now?"

Tom: I value what I don't have...in this moment.

Jake: Health?

Tom: Yes, health. Freedom. Going for a run. Mowing the lawn.

Jake: I understand. So often we don't know what we value until we lose it. Some people know, but they don't necessarily live according to their values. Then there's a small group—at least in my experience—who know what they value and live by those values.

Tom: I know a few people like that.

Jake: My guess is that they stand out among the people you know. People who live in accordance with their highest values have discovered one way to minimize the existential angst that you and I discussed. Their lives have a sense of purpose and direction. They live a chosen life. I meet very few people who actually live this way.

In the workshops I've conducted in America and Japan, I guide participants through a process in which they discover their top values. Very few people even know what their most important values are and even fewer can say, "I live according to what I truly value."

Tom: How do you help people figure out their values?

Jake: There's a whole process that I take people through, but here's the essence of it. To know what we value, we only need to see what it is that we work hard to gain or to keep in our lives. It's because of our values that we take action, either to acquire something or to preserve what we have. Follow someone around for a week or two, watch what they do, and you'll learn what they value.

But then, notice if there's a difference between what they say they value and how they live their lives. They may say they value health, but every time there is a choice to do something healthy or do something to make more money, they choose to make money. This person values money, or what money does for them, over health. Another person says she values spending time with her son, but whenever she's with her son she's talking on her cell phone to a girlfriend. She actually values social contact over spending time with her son. I perceive these people as being incongruent because they don't live according to what they say they value. They're living according to outdated habits, or outdated values, or possibly they're living according to someone else's values. This kind of incongruity hinders our growth.

Tom: But a lot of people live that way.

Jake: Yes, but are they **re**newing themselves? Do they allow themselves to **re**create their lives—to update their values and behaviors?

Tom: You think if we live according to what we truly value we'll be happier?

Jake: I think that's often the case, but there are situations where living according to our values can be challenging.

Tom: Then what do we do?

Jake: We do what we do. We each grapple with our choices. I don't think there's any formula to follow. When we have a serious conflict in our lives it's often because our values are in conflict with one another. If value X were clearly the better value to live by, compared to value Y, we wouldn't have a conflict. The conflict arises because both X and Y seem to have merit. And they both have costs associated with them.

Tom: I know how that feels.

Jake: So do I.

Tom: How do you deal with those situations in your life?

Jake: I ask myself, "What's the guiding principle in my life? What is my overarching value, the value that I choose to set the tone for my whole life?" For some people the answer is security, for others it's goodness or generosity, for others it's power, which is a form of security for many people. For some people it's love, or justice, or personal growth, and on and on.

Tom: For you?

Jake: Beauty. What I value most is finding beauty in my life, the people, the places, my work, my clients; whatever I'm doing I want to find the beauty. When I see the beauty in a person, I'm sure to interact with them in a respectful way. I sustain myself —feed myself—by interacting with people in a respectful way.

I have a ritual I do that helps me connect with my guiding principle. Every night I go outside and look at the North Star and ask myself, "Have I experienced beauty today?" I do this as a simple way to hold myself accountable.

Tom: Why the North Star?

Jake: Because I always know where it is, no matter if clouds or snow or rain obscure it, the North Star is a constant. And so is my desire to treat people in a respectful manner...to find beauty.

Tom: It's nice for me to hear you talk about yourself this way. I'm not sure I ever thought about beauty as a value. I'll have to think about what my guiding principle or highest value is. Do you think there are any universal values?

Jake: Not really. I see our values as being dependent upon the context of our lives. Our values evolve as we age, as our consciousness shifts, and as our circumstances change. Sometimes when people share the same context, they share similar values. Take a hundred people, put them all in the same context where their basic needs are met, give them all a high level of consciousness, and I suppose they may live peacefully. Maybe their highest value would be cooperation. Take the same hundred people and place them in a situation with limited resources, without enough food or water for all of them to survive, and I suspect that different values would emerge.

Tom: You don't inspire hope.

Jake: You mean you don't inspire hope with my words? I do. I find hope because I believe that we can alter the context of our lives. Many of us have a good chance of creating a context in which we can live according to our chosen values.

Tom: What about valuing life over death, isn't that a universal value?

Jake: I don't think so. Some people choose euthanasia because they value relief over life—a life of pain. The suicide bombers in the Middle East value martyrdom over life. A parent may sacrifice their life for their child's life because they value the life of their child over their own.

Tom: So, you're saying that all values are subjective and they depend on the situations in which we find ourselves?

Jake: Yes. Our values are statements about what we each hold as important. And what's important varies depending upon our life circumstances, our stage of development, and the evolution of our Identity.

Tom: I agree with that. I suppose it's why different people respond in different ways to a life-threatening crisis. And why one person may respond in different ways at different times, depending on what's going on in his life.

Jake: I've had individuals come into my office who were dealing with serious health crises, life-threatening challenges like yours, and they respond in remarkably different ways. One person may accept their illness and take no action to stop it. Another person may go into denial. Another may assume responsibility for having created their illness and then make significant lifestyle changes to overcome their illness.

Tom: Do you think people create their illnesses?

Jake: Sometimes, but not always. I mean some people just don't take care of themselves. Other people try to take really good care of themselves, like you, but there are so many factors that contribute to creating illness. I think we need to be very careful about suggesting that people are always responsible for their illnesses or other negative things that happen to them.

Tom: I'm surprised to hear you say that because you're such a proponent of self-responsibility.

Jake: Yes, take responsibility for how we deal with what happens to us, but we're not always responsible for what happens.

Tom: Even when people get sick I suppose taking responsibility is better than going into denial.

Jake: Actually there's medical research demonstrating that a period of denial is one of the most effective ways to deal with news of life-threatening illnesses. So there's even a time for denial. Sometimes we just need a break from reality. The research says that denial is an effective initial response, but then there comes a stage in which people need to come out of denial.

Tom: But the thrust of everything you believe in is that it's better when we take responsibility for ourselves.

Jake: Yes, taking responsibility is what I believe in and that includes the responsibility to live according to what we value.

Tom: Do you know people who consistently live this way?

Jake: Enough to know that it's possible. And based on the time I spent with John and Joyce Weir, I'm certain that living this way means you'll make the most of your life. They practiced the things you and I've been talking about. They used **Re**Speak. They fully individuated. They understood and took responsibility for their limiting core patterns, and for the emotional footprints they left behind. And they lived according to their values.

They consciously lived their lives. They kept growing. That's how they **re**newed themselves. They pursued activities that gave them great pleasure and satisfaction. When I met them, they were both eighty-five years old. John referred to that age-stage as "self-actualized." He said the primary task in that stage of life is to prepare for death so that you can consciously die. He believed in doing everything consciously.

They were a great example of two individuals who became a team without losing their individuality. In some ways, even after sixty years of marriage, they still appeared to be curious about each other. They certainly didn't always agree. When they didn't, they would take some time to understand each other's point of view, to witness each other, and then they seemed to move on instead of pressing to create common ground.

They were the most relaxed yet engaged people I've ever been around. Whatever they were doing, they were doing fully. When

John lectured, even if the audience appeared bored, John seemed to delight himself in his own experience. When eating, they were eating, talking about the food, fully engaged in the experience.

We went to a restaurant with John and Joyce when we visited them in Morro Bay. John went up to the hostess to put our party's name on the wait list and when the hostess asked John his name he said, "My name's Jake Eagle." When I asked him why he used my name he said he thought I had a great name and he wanted to experience what it would be like to have my name. He was always curious and he acted on his curiosity in a playful way.

At the end of that meal, John ordered a huge piece of mud pie for dessert. When some of the other people at the table wanted a bite he refused to give them any. He said he wanted to eat the entire thing; he'd been looking forward to it all morning. He said that if other people wanted some they should order their own. They said they couldn't eat an entire piece of pie, and John told them to order it anyway, and what they couldn't eat, he'd eat. And he did. He delighted in every bite. I think he spent half an hour just eating dessert.

After we left the restaurant, we drove around and around in circles in the parking lot. John was showing me the turning radius of his new hybrid car that he was so excited about. He was like a kid, taking such pleasure in his experience. He said he had come "full circle" in his life, from the first car he had in the 1920s, which was powered with electricity stored in batteries.

Tom: They sound pretty lively for people preparing to die. Tell me more about how they prepared to consciously die.

Jake: Preparing to consciously die isn't necessarily about imminent death. It's a process that can extend over many years. During the process we **re**arrange our values and priorities, we focus on completion, we live more and more in the present moment. It's another step in our process of growth that requires awareness, acceptance, asking, awaiting, and then acting.

Tom: Maybe it's the one time we await and don't have to act.

Jake: I don't know. Wouldn't it be great to choose the moment?

Tom: Sure, how about in fifty years?

Jake: Yeah, that sounds good.

Tom: Did John or Joyce want to live longer than they did?

Jake: John seemed completely fascinated with his own process of decline and very accepting of whatever was happening. At the last workshop John ever conducted, he was still discovering things about himself. But more and more, he was discovering his own physical limitations. Instead of being upset by this, he expressed his new awareness as if he'd discovered some gem.

Tom: He wasn't distressed to discover his physical limitations?

John: No, he was intrigued. I remember him telling us how he was reverting to some infant-like qualities, such as not being able to turn himself over. One day he told me that he realized that when he lost a capability, I think he was talking about physical capabilities, that he would never get it back. The lost capability was now part of who John Weir had become. It wasn't something to resist or try to restore.

Tom: What age was he when he told you that?

Jake: That's a good point. He was in his late eighties. It's not as though John prematurely gave into the process of aging. He was still jogging at the age of eighty. But my point is that once he did start to lose various abilities, he didn't resist, he was accepting and curious.

Tom: And he wasn't afraid to die, not anxious about it?

Jake: No, not at all. He even told me that he was pretty sure how he'd die. He described the process in quite a bit of detail.

Tom: I wonder if his fearlessness and curiosity were the result of his philosophy about life, or do you think it just comes with growing old and naturally becoming more accepting?

Jake: Look at most of the elders we know, they don't necessarily expand and grow more curious with age. I perceive John and Joyce's lack of anxiety about death as a direct result of the way they lived, and the way they lived was an example of **Re**ology.

They lived outside the limitations of dualistic thinking. No good/bad, right/wrong labels. They lived in the now. John and Joyce took complete responsibility for themselves—no victimization at all. They never fretted about things being unfair. They were very aware and engaged with life, accepting whatever was going on—responding appropriately, and continuing to deepen themselves.

And the way they spoke—using **Re**Speak—is a huge part of their story. This is number four of the four things I mentioned earlier when I was saying I boil all of this down to four things we can do to live healthier lives. Using **Re**Speak breaks us out of dualistic thinking. We empower ourselves with this language. We bring ourselves into the now. We see possibility instead of peril. I can't stress enough how central this was in their lives.

Tom: Very unusual people. The way you describe them and their way of being in the world is so very different from what most of us experience.

Jake: It is a fundamentally different way of being in the world.

Tom: The juxtaposition of living fully and dying consciously is very interesting to me.

Jake: How so?

Tom: Well, living and dying seem like opposites. At times, I think that being aware of my death impinges on living. But as I listen to you, I also understand that being aware of my eventual death encourages me to live more fully, if I have the time.

Jake: When I think too much about death I can depress myself, particularly when I think of losing the people I love. But if I don't think about death at all, I lose a certain edge, I take things for granted. I have this idea that if we really truly become comfortable with death, we could think about it without scaring ourselves. We all have our time on earth. We come and we go, like waves on the beach. When I think about death in that way I feel pretty relaxed, but I just haven't gotten to the point where I think about death that way all the time. I continue to experience some anxiety around death. I remember talking to John about this. It was during a time when Joyce moved to a nursing home and John told me, "She and I can no longer take care of her without professional assistance."

I said something to him like, "I imagine you must be sad and that this must be terribly hard for Joyce."

He said, "I don't ask questions such as, 'What's this like for Joyce?' because I can't possibly know. As for me, I'm not sad because I'm not comparing the current situation to the way things used to be. When I do that, I miss out on what's going on now.

"When I visit Joyce, sometimes she's available and sometimes she doesn't even recognize me. If she's available, we connect. If she's not, we don't."

Tom: Pretty extraordinary.

Jake: I agree. Shortly after John and I had that conversation I visited Dad, who for the first time in my life was shorter than me. I realized he was becoming a shrinking part of me. He seemed somewhat frail. But because of my conversation with John, I was able to be with Dad as he was, without comparing him to how he used to be. As a result, I thoroughly enjoyed the way we were together. His humor was wonderful, just delivered more slowly. His wisdom was still apparent. He said to me that he'd come to believe that people are just who they are and we might as well accept them. Pretty good, eh?

Tom: That's what I said earlier.

Jake: Puts you in good company.

Tom: True.

Jake: My life feels more potent when I accept aging and dying as part of life. Hannah and I were driving to a movie the other day and I said to her, "This is it. This is our life. There is no place we're going, other than to a movie, and there's no place we're waiting to arrive. This is it. This is us."

Tom: This is me.

CHAPTER 18

A Conversation to Cherish

The next day when I showed up at the hospital, thinking we'd continue our conversation, I found that Tom was much less alert than he had been during my last visit. He spoke sparingly, using fewer words, saying only what really mattered. I cherish everything he said to me that day.

Jake: After I return from Tokyo I'm planning to come back to Maine for a week. Will you be here?

Tom: I don't know. I'm really tired, Jake. But it's important for the family to love each other.

Jake: We are, and what you're going through is bringing everyone closer.

He raised his eyebrows and grunted, which I perceived to mean, "Did I have to get sick for everyone to come together?"

Jake: Hey, I went to Rand's hockey game last night. He was incredible; I wish you could have seen him.

Tom: I have. I know what you're talking about. I love that about him.

Jake: His team won 13-0. On and off the ice he was really impressive the way he handled himself.

Tom: Like you.

I paused. I had never felt such appreciation from my brother. I wanted to stop time—to hold the moment. At some point I discomforted myself with the silence and I continued.

Jake: Is there anything I can do for you?

Tom: I'm sorry.

Jake: You don't need to be.

I knew I should just witness Tom, but my knee-jerk response was so strong. I wanted to help him feel better.

Tom: Your house is great.

Jake: Thanks. We're really happy with it.

Tom: No, I mean it's really great. Forget about how I said you could do things to make it better. It's great.

Jake: I'm so glad you saw it.

He just nodded his head in affirmation.

Tom: Hannah's an unusual lady—solid, special. You're a really lucky man.

Jake: I know.

There was a long pause.

Tom: If I can do anything for you when you're in Tokyo, let me know.

Jake: Thanks, I will.

Tom's offer to help me was the last thing he ever said to me. His words felt like those of a big brother, a role that I believe he wanted to play in my life. After he spoke those words, he seemed to drift in and out of sleep as I rubbed his neck. I stood there, quietly talking to him, realizing we might never talk again.

Jake: Can you hear me, Tom? I want you to know that because of our conversation, I'm even more committed to practicing this way of living that you and I have been talking about. Many of my ideas about life and death have been tested in the time we've spent together since you became ill. I've come to see that dying and truth-telling are companions. Dying creates immediacy, so truth-telling becomes imperative. As time evaporates, the haze seems to clear, and I know what I need to say. I see myself—both of us—in a stark, simple way.

Tommy, why did it take such a crisis for us to be able to connect? For my part, it's because I've spent much of my life judging you and being unwilling to fully reveal myself because I was afraid I'd be rejected. Instead of taking responsibility for myself, I judged you so that I could justify not reaching out to you. I see what I've cost myself as a result of holding back.

Why hold back? With you, holding back became a habit. In the beginning I gave you a lot of power because you were my older brother. I tried several times to reach out to you, but when we didn't agree, I always pulled back instead of gracefully accepting our differences. The past couple of years I've done better. And only now, when you're so ill, have we found a new way to connect. I'm convinced we could have had such conversations without this crisis, and broken our pattern, but to do so required courage.

I never fully showed myself, so how could you have seen me? I'm absolutely sure that the solution to freeing ourselves from our habitual ways is to reveal ourselves in the present moment. Don't wait for the right time. Don't anticipate what will happen. Don't compare one thing to another. Just show up, right now, in this moment. It's not complicated, but not always easy.

Do you hear me, Tommy?

He squeezed my hand twice.

The last time I saw Tom he was in the hospital, sleeping, looking restful. I kept looking at him until he looked beautiful in my eyes, knowing that it might be a final image.

Hannah and I returned to New Mexico and a few days later Tom left the hospital. He went back to his home where his family, our sister, her son, and our parents cared for him. When it was necessary, hospice workers were called upon to provide the care that they specialize in.

I left for my annual trip to work in Tokyo. On my way I stopped to rest in Honolulu for a few days and while I was there my sister, Lizabeth, called to tell me that Tommy had died. He had been surrounded by everyone in the family, except for Hannah and me. When I called Hannah to tell her, we cried and cried. Knowing he was going to die wasn't the same as having him die.

The most searing part of my experience is the finality of death. That's it! Over—no more chances, no corrections, no what ifs, nothing more. When I look at Tom's picture, which I do every day since he died, I say, "That was your life. You got those fifty-six years and did what you did with them. That's it. That's you. Each of us will do what we do with our lives. Because of you, I'm making more of mine. Because of the brevity of your life I'm more awake for each extra day of mine."

Epilogue

Tom was the president of a very unique organization in Maine that hosts an annual conference for thought leaders from all over the world. It's like a smaller, more intimate version of the TED (Technology, Entertainment, Design) conference that takes place on the West Coast. Hundreds of participants gather every fall and talk about the remarkable things that are happening around the world, and the ways in which individuals can make a meaningful difference in the lives of other people. As a tribute to my brother's interest in encouraging us to be "global citizens," I want to say a few words about the larger perspective of how altering our language can alter not only our personal worlds, but also the greater world we live in.

Reology compels us to evolve from an ego-centered perspective to an ethno-centered perspective, and from an ethno-centered to a world-centered perspective. When we interpret events with ourselves as the primary point of reference, this is an ego-centered stance. If we interpret events with our tribe or community as our primary point of reference, this is an ethno-centered stance. If we interpret events with humanity as our primary point of reference, this is a world-centered stance.

When we're born, we don't have a sense of self. We haven't yet differentiated our self; we're still unformed. Then we grow into our sense of self, and as part of forming our self we enter the stage of egocentricity. At this stage our priority is self. If we experience a high level of stress, our point of reference becomes "me against the world." Many children remain in an egocentric stance until their teenaged years. Some people remain there longer.

But generally, by the time we're in our teens, we start to become ethnocentric. We still have our egocentric orientation, but we add an ethnocentric orientation. We become aware of and interested in other people. We're interested in being part of a tribe, a group, or a community. Our point of reference includes consideration of and connection with our tribe. When under stress, we no longer frame events as "me against the world." Instead, we frame them as "my tribe against your tribe."

With this perspective we believe our religion is the true religion, whatever "religion" we believe in—even the religion of atheism. In this stage, we identify with a select group of people, and we have a strong tendency to view those who are not part of our tribe as potential threats.

If we continue to evolve, which presently only a small percentage of the population does, we may develop to the point of becoming world-centered. We continue to have our egocentric and ethno-centric perspective, but we add to those by developing a world-centered perspective. This is when our point of reference expands and includes all people, and all points of view. We no longer frame things as "my tribe against your tribe" because we respect the different ways that different people have of making meaning. When we have a world-centered point of reference, we realize that everyone sees the world in his or her own way. Our attachment to any one perspective loosens up, and we enter the world of pluralism in which we understand and appreciate people's differences.

A person who has only developed an egocentric orientation sees the world from his perspective and thinks other people see it from his perspective as well. When he walks into a room full of people he thinks that all the other people are aware of him. The egocentric person has a singular perspective. A person who has developed to a world-centered orientation sees the world from their perspective and realizes that everyone else sees the world from their own unique perspective. When she walks into a room she is aware that everyone else in that room is as preoccupied with their personal experience as she is with hers. The world-centered person has a pluralistic perspective.

ReSpeak is a world-centered, pluralistic language, which propels us toward higher stages of human development. ReSpeak elevates the level of our consciousness and the level of our conversations.

I'm convinced that as a species, we urgently need to move in the direction of a world-centered perspective or our species may deprive itself of any future at all. Without this advance in consciousness, a great many people will continue to suffer violence and experience the conflicts that arise from too tightly holding an egocentric or ethno-centric point of view. These points of view cannot be eliminated. They are necessary steps in our development—to be accepted and honored—but best viewed as stages of development that we grow through.

Just as ReSpeak directs our development, so too does the ordinary use of language; it just directs us in a different way. Whatever language we use will hinder or hasten our development. Ordinary language will hinder our development when we use it to diminish those who differ from us; ReSpeak will hasten our development because it dignifies our differences.

The egocentric and ethnocentric points of view discourage us from accepting full responsibility for ourselves. It's easy for us to victimize ourselves with an egocentric point of view: "Look at what they're doing to me." It's easy for us to victimize ourselves with an ethnocentric point of view: "Look at what they're doing to us." But with ReSpeak, all I can say is: "Look at what I'm doing to myself," or collectively: "Look at what we're doing to ourselves."

When we engage with people from a world-centered perspective, we naturally experience more empathy and, as a result, more intimacy and less conflict. We naturally learn and grow by expanding our Identity through exposure and openness to ideas that differ from our own.

Learning **Re**Speak requires effort and takes time. But as I recently heard someone say, "All real meaning in this world accrues in duration. Our work and our relationships benefit from sustained attention." The practice of **Re**Speak does require sustained attention. John Weir used to say that it takes five years to completely alter our language patterns. My experience more or less bears that out. The practice of **Re**Speak is not a quick fix. That's why we call it a practice. And like any practice, this one requires commitment. I think of this as a way of living. Every time I speak, all day long, I have a clear choice. I can speak as a victim, justifying myself, or I can speak as a creator—the one creating my life.

Postscript

The inscription at the beginning of this book is to my wife, Hannah. It reads, "Beauty framed by impermanence." Thanks to this journey I traveled with Tom, the beauty that I find in my life is now enhanced by my awareness of its impermanence.

While writing this book I struggled with questions about death and the meaning of life, questions that were amplified in the midst of loss and grief when Hannah's sister, Sarah, was killed in a hit-and-run auto accident eleven months before Tom was diagnosed with a brain tumor. Then came Tom's death followed by my father's, exactly one year to the day after my brother's diagnosis.

During and after these losses, I immersed myself in my feelings and thoughts about death. I sought answers to my questions, reading existential psychology books, spiritual texts, and autobiographies of wise old people who had survived tragedies. I spoke with others who had lost a loved one, hoping to find some guidance, and I went into therapy to explore my feelings. It is also during this time that I completed the writing of this book.

Through this entire process, I came to realize that my awareness of death presents me with an opportunity to more fully live my life. But to do so, I need to feel death's poignancy without becoming preoccupied with death.

Below, I share some of my personal experiences—ways I hindered myself and ways I helped myself—as I grappled with losing loved ones. I hope my words may be helpful to others who are also searching for ways to cope with loss.

TIME:

I have experienced the truism that time heals. One of my
mentors, a smart and thoughtful man, told me that grief is
optional. I never lightly dismiss any of his comments but my
experience shows me that the ties that bind us to our loved
ones, the habits that become so familiar, the identity of "us," the
expectations of having someone in our lives when we wake up
tomorrow—these deeply embedded experiences take time to
transform from grief into memories.

The first two weeks after each of my loved ones died was the
time when I most severely disoriented myself. Barely allowing
myself to breathe, I felt detached from the world; I wanted
everything to stop to honor these people I loved, but it didn't.
As a result, I felt pretty much alone, only connected with others
who also shared the loss.

But as the second week passed, even though I still felt detached,
a distinct shift occurred. I no longer lived solely in the world of
grief. I had to go back to work, to prepare for future
commitments, and these demands were like a bridge back to my
life. I lived in two worlds for a while—maybe a couple of
months. During that time I connected more than usual with my
family members. I talked and thought more about the deceased
than I did when they were alive. But I also started to laugh
again, to allow myself to enjoy myself, and to dream about my
future.

With each death my responses were different. I shocked myself
because of the suddenness of my sister-in-law's death. I not only
saddened myself about losing Sarah, but also angered and
bewildered myself with thoughts about the man who killed her.
I pained myself with regret when my brother died. I experienced
relief when my father died; his health was declining and I just
couldn't bear the thought of him suffering.

After the first couple of months there was another distinct shift —more relief—but many questions remained: I wondered how we—family and friends—would cope? Would we return to our old patterns of relating with one another or would our new patterns of relating last? Would we make meaningful changes in our lives, or would we drift back to our old habits?

The one-year anniversary of each death brought some perspective and marked a milestone in the process of facing death. My questions about how we would cope had been answered. All of us had coped, but each in our own ways. Other questions had not been answered, but I stopped trying to answer them.

Ways I Hindered Myself and Caused Myself More Pain:

After the premature deaths of Sarah and Tom, I pained myself by trying to imagine how Sarah and Tom might feel about their own deaths. I'm aware that there is something odd about this question because the deceased do not examine their own deaths —not as far as I know—but I kept imagining how they would feel and I thought they would be very upset, particularly my brother. While Sarah had been satisfied with the life she lived, my sense is that my brother had not been. In retrospect I see that I was trying to stay connected to those I lost by projecting my feelings about death onto them. I created my own unnecessary drama and stuck myself in the past, hindering my ability to be fully alive in the present.

I also trapped myself in these tragedies by asking a number of "what if" questions that took me back in time, back to a place in which I pained myself and found no answers.

What if the man who had hit and killed Sarah had turned around and come back to help her? How could she not have seen the oncoming car? Had she been distracted? Was the driver unaware or malicious? I wondered what Tom would have done had he had more time and more capacity to direct the last few weeks of his life. I wondered about the choices he might have made had he known his life would be cut short.

While these kinds of questions may be necessary for a short period of time to help us sift through our confusion that arises from untimely deaths, at some point they become a distraction from life.

The other way I hindered myself was by thinking that if I were too joyous—too happy—I wasn't honoring Tom. I now perceive this to be a misuse of his death. I have come to believe the best way I can honor my brother is make the most of the days I have. I now celebrate every day I am alive.

WAYS I HELPED MYSELF AND RECONNECTED WITH MY HOPE AND OPTIMISM:

Early on in my grief, I began to practice the following meditation: I sit and think about all the people and animals I love. After I visualize each one, I say to myself that we each will die. I say each person's name and the words "will die." So, it sounds like this: "I will die, Hannah will die, Mom will die, Lizabeth will die, Chama will die, Jennifer will die, Ashley will die, Alexander will die, Shar will die, Maow will die, all of my clients will die…" I grounded myself with these meditations, normalizing death, accepting death, the undeniable. In doing so I calmed myself.

I also helped myself deal with my fear of Hannah's death, by envisioning my life without her. I pictured myself living alone in our house, cooking my own meals, buying the groceries, traveling alone on vacation. I saw myself driving alone, hiking alone, working with people, and caring for our pets. I was able to create in my mind a future without Hannah. By doing so I comforted myself.

Finally, I helped myself—but not for a while—by becoming realistic about the potential of each of these relationships. Shortly after their deaths I had a tendency to romanticize what could have been. Over time I could acknowledge what was positive, as well as our struggles, our differences, and our incompatibilities. By being realistic about the ways we related—with no praise and no blame—I created more peace for myself.

PREPARING FOR DEATH:

Neither my brother nor my father prepared for death. My father never talked about it. My brother only began to discuss it when he was too tired and too ill to do some of the things he would have done had he prepared sooner. While my father and brother didn't leave letters behind, my sister-in-law did and this was remarkably helpful. She wrote clearly about her life. She stated that if we were reading the letter it meant she had died. She shared with those she left behind her thoughts and feelings about her life. She told us how she wanted us to remember her and think about her.

When those of us who are left behind know what the deceased person wants us to do, we can stop asking the unanswerable questions. This makes it easier for us to honor them. I encourage you to write a letter, and update it every few years. Let people know:

§ Whatever you want them to know.

§ How you want your loved ones to honor you.

§ After you die, do you want their world to stop? For a day, three days, a year, forever, not at all?

§ Or, do you want them to laugh, to go for walks, even go back to watching TV? And if so, when? The day you die, not for a day, a week, a month, a year, never?

§ And, how do you want them to remember you?

I was going to write, "In the end what matters..." but it isn't just the end that matters, it's every day that we are alive. Death teaches us to use our limited time wisely, living every day according to our deepest values, growing until the moment we die, and creating and leaving behind emotional footprints we are proud of.

With the ideas presented in this book I have created an understanding of life and death for myself. I comfort myself. I ground myself. I compel myself to fully live my life. I hope you find ways to help yourself with these ideas and words. And remember, the way you use the words may be as important as the words you use.

APPENDIX A

What follows are a wide range of examples of **Re**Speak. The strike-through portion eliminates the use of regular language and the italicized portion show the conversion to **Re**Speak. Each of these sentences was used in this book, but here you can see the contrast of regular language compared to **Re**Speak.

~~They~~ *I* will change and evolve, but this is me now.

~~I feel limited~~ *I limit myself* by my own immaturity, but I don't blame my ego for that.

But ~~it helps me~~ *I help myself* a great deal when I think that…

~~This concerns me~~ *I concern myself…*

I never get rid of ~~it~~ *myself*; I just build upon ~~it~~ *myself.*

Ever since then ~~I've been fascinated~~ *I fascinate myself* with the power and pervasiveness of repression…

~~I was disoriented~~ *I disoriented myself* with anxiety.

I was successful and rewarded by our culture, but ~~I was exhausted~~ *I exhausted myself.*

When I experience that felt-sense, ~~it helps~~ *I help myself* if I express myself in a way that acknowledges what I'm experiencing.

Don't you think that most of the time ~~we get hurt~~ *we hurt ourselves* because we haven't been honest all along?

But since we can't kill our existential angst, and we can't run from it—because "it" is us—we repress ~~it~~ *ourselves.*

She's my partner and I accept that ~~her actions will often impact me~~ *I will often impact myself with her actions.*

If ~~I am surprised by her actions~~ *I surprise myself by her actions,* then I imagine that I've fallen asleep at the wheel and have not been paying attention to the warning signs along the way.

If I didn't love you well before, there are consequences, but I have a chance to correct ~~it~~ *myself.*

~~These ideas depressed me~~ *I depressed myself with these ideas,* but like many people, I missed the important point.

~~It may have served us well~~ *We may have served ourselves well* when we developed our pattern…

If we learn to see our core pattern—and take responsibility for ~~it~~ *ourselves*—we can heal our relationship with our pasts and grow ourselves up.

You always have access to your own nervous system, which means you can influence ~~it~~ *yourself* and work with ~~it~~ *yourself*—attend to yourself.

Without healthy beliefs, ones that promote hope, we're apt ~~to suffer from depression~~ *to depress ourselves.*

I took responsibility for ~~them~~ *myself* and ~~they~~ *I* calmed down because these parts of me were witnessed instead of being hidden away.

Eventually, ~~they'll disappoint you~~ *you'll disappoint yourself.*

If your partner gives too much, you'll become dependent. If she doesn't give enough you'll ~~be frustrated~~ *frustrate yourself.*

She never created appropriate emotional boundaries, so ~~she was held hostage~~ *she held herself hostage* by other people's nervous systems.

2 Rules of ReSpeak

Rule # 1: **Re**Turn To Now

Rule # 2: **Re**Move Praise and Blame

2 Guidelines of ReSpeak

Guideline # 1: **Re**Source Your Feelings

"I <u>am delighting</u> myself."

"I <u>frustrate</u> myself."

"I <u>make myself</u> sad."

Guideline # 2: **Re**Spect Our Differences

"I perceive _____ as _____."

APPENDIX C

THE 5 STEPS OF GROWTH

Awareness

Acceptance

Asking

Awaiting

Acting

Bibliography

Abram, David, *The Spell of the Sensuous*, New York: Vintage Books, 1997

Ackerman, Diane, *Natural History of the Senses*, New York: Vintage Books, 1991

Ames, Joan Evelyn, *Mastery: Interviews with 30 Remarkable People*, Portland: Rudra Press, 1997

Beck, Don, *Spiral Dynamics: Mastering Values, Leadership, and Change*, Malden, MA: Blackwell Publishing Ltd, 1996

Branden, Nathaniel, *Honoring The Self*, New York: Bantam Books, 1983

-------------, *The Disowned Self*, New York: Bantam Books, 1972

-------------, *Breaking Free*, New York: Bantam Books, 1970

-------------, *Taking Responsibility*, New York: Fireside, 1996

-------------, *If you could hear what I cannot say*, Bantam Books, 1983

-------------, *Judgment Day: My Years with Ayn Rand*, Boston: Houghton Mifflin Company, 1989

Brann, Eva, *Plato's Phaedo*, Newburyport, MA: Focus Publishing, 1998

Burrow, Trigant, *The Neurosis of Man*, New York: Philosophical Library, 1953

Callahan, Gerald N., *Faith, Madness, and Spontaneous Human Combustion*, New York: St. Martin's Press, 2002

Carter, Rita, *Mapping the Mind*, Los Angeles: University of California Press, Ltd, 1999

Carter, Forest, *The Education of Little Tree*, Albuquerque: University of New Mexico Press, 1976

Childre, Doc, *The Heartmath Solution*, New York: HarperCollins, 1999

Chilton Pearce, Joseph, *Magical Child*, New York: Penguin Books, 1992

------------, *The Biology of Transcendence: A Blueprint of the Human Spirit*, Rochester, VT: Park Street Press, 2002

Cialdini, Robert B., *Influence: The Psychology of Persuasion*, New York: William Morrow and Company, Inc, 1993

Covey, Stephen R., *The 7 Habits of Highly Effective People*, New York: Fireside, 1989

Cytowic, Richard E., *The Man Who Tasted Shapes*, New York: G. P. Putnam's Sons, 1993

Damasio, Antonio R., *Descartes' Error: Emotion, Reason, and the Human Brain*, New York: Avon Books, 1995

de Botton, Alain, *Statue Anxiety*, New York: Pantheon Books, 2004

Diamond, Louise, *The Courage for Peace: Daring to Create Harmony in Ourselves and the World*, Berkeley: Conari Press, 2000

Dozier, Jr., Rush W., *Fear Itself*, New York: Thomas Dunne Books, 1998

Dychtwald, Ken, *Bodymind*, Los Angeles: Jeremy P. Tarcher, Inc., 1977

Erikson, Erik H., *Identity and the Life Cycle*, New York: W.W. Norton & Company, 1980

Feynman, Richard P., *The Meaning of It All: Thoughts of a Citizen Scientist*, Reading, MA: Perseus Books, 1998

Friedman, Thomas L., *The Lexus and the Olive Tree*, New York: Anchor Books, 2000

Gaines, Jack, *Fritz Perls: Here & Now*, Millbrae, CA: Celestial Arts, 1979

Gerrold, David, *Worlds of Wonder: How to Write Science Fiction & Fantasy*, Cincinnati: Writer's Digest Books, 2001

Gladwell, Malcolm, *Blink: The Power of Thinking Without Thinking*, New York: Little, Brown and Company, 2005

Glasser, William, *Choice Theory: A New Psychology of Personal Freedom*, New York: HarperCollins, 1998

Goleman, Daniel, *Vital Lies, Simple Truths: The Psychology of Self-Deception*, New York: Simon & Schuster, 1983

------------, *Emotional Intelligence*, New York: Bantam Books, 1995

Greenspan, Stanley I., *The Growth of the Mind*, Reading, MA: Perseus Books, 1997

--------------, *The First Idea: How Symbols, Language, and Intelligence Evolved From Our Primate Ancestors to Modern Humans*, Cambridge: Da Capo Press, 2004

Haley, Alex, *The Autobiography of Malcolm X*, New York: Ballantine Publishing Group, 1964

Hammer, Leon, *Dragon Rises, Red Bird Flies*, Barrytown, NY: Station Hill Press, 1990

Hampden-Turner, Charles, *Maps of the Mind*, New York: Macmillan Publishing Company, 1982

Hanna, Thomas, *The Body of Life*, Rochester, VT: Healing Arts Press, 1979

Harris, Thomas, *Hannibal*, New York: Delacorte Press, 1999

--------------, *Red Dragon*, New York: Dell Publishing, 1981

Hayakawa, S.I., *Language in Thought and Action*, Orlando, FL: Harcourt, Inc., 1990

Heaton, John, *Wittgenstein for Beginners*, Cambridge, England: Icon Books, Ltd., 1994

Herrigel, Eugen, *Zen in the Art of Archery*, New York: Vintage Books, 1999

Horney, Karen, *Neurosis and Human Growth*, New York: W.W. Norton & Company, 1950

Howard, Pierce J., *The Owner's Manual for the Brain*, Austin: Leornian Press, 1994

Howarth, David, *We Die Alone: A WWII Epic of Escape and Endurance*, New York: Lyons Press, 1999

Huxley, Aldous, *The Perennial Philosophy*, New York: Harper and Row, Publishers, 1944

Jaims, Mikel, *Flight of a Golden Eagle*, Mesa, AZ: Golden Eagle Wellness Foundation, 1989

James, William, *A Pluralistic Universe*, Lincoln: University of Nebraska Press, 1996

Jaynes, Julian, *The Origin of Consciousness in the Breakdown of the Bicameral Mind*, Boston: Houghton Mifflin Company, 1982

Johnson, Crockett, *Harold and the Purple Crayon*, New York: HarperCollins, 1955

Keen, Sam, *Learning to Fly: Trapeze - Reflections on Fear, Trust, and the Joy of Letting Go*, New York: Broadway Books, 1999

King, Martin Luther, *I Have a Dream*, Washington, DC, August 28, 1963

Klein, Gary, *Sources of Power: How People Make Decisions*, Cambridge: MIT Press, 1998

Kohn, Alfie, *Punished by Rewards: The Trouble with Gold Stars, Incentive Plans, A's, Praise, and Other Bribes*, New York: Houghton Mifflin Company, 1993

Kotre, John, *Season of Life: The Dramatic Journey from Birth to Death*, Ann Arbor: University of Michigan Press, 1990

Kottler, Jeffrey A., *On Being a Therapist*, San Francisco: Jossey-Bass, Inc., 1993

Krell, David Farrell, Editor, *Martin Heidegger: Basic Writings*, New York: HarperCollins, 1993

Krishnamurti, *The Flight of the Eagle*, New York: Harper and Row, Publishers, 1972

Krishnamurti, *The First and Last Freedom*, New York: HarperCollins, 1975

Lakoff, Robin Tolmach, *The Language War*, Los Angeles: University of California Press, Ltd, 2000

Leary, Timothy, *Flashbacks: A Personal and Cultural History of an Era*, Los Angeles: Jeremy P. Tarcher, Inc., 1990

LeDoux, Joseph, *The Emotional Brain: The Mysterious Underpinnings of Emotional Life*, New York: Simon & Schuster, 1996

LeDoux, Joseph, *Synaptic Self: How Our Brains Become Who We Are*, New York: Viking, 2002

Levine, Peter A., *Waking the Tiger: Healing Trauma*, Berkeley: North Atlantic Books, 1997

Loevinger, Jane, *Paradigms of Personality*, New York: W. H. Freeman and Company, 1987

Loman, Susan, *The Body-Mind Connection in Human Movement Analysis*, Keene, NH: Antioch New England Graduate School, 1992

Lowen, Alexander, *The Language of the Body*, New York: Collier Books, 1971

Lowen, Alexander, *Narcissism: Denial of the True Self*, New York: Touchstone, 1997

Lowen, Alexander, *Bioenergetics: The Revolutionary Therapy That Uses the Language of The Body to Heal the Problems of the Mind*, New York: Penguin Books, 1975

Lowen, Alexander, *The Way to Vibrant Health: A Manual of Bioenergetic Exercises*, New York: Harper Colophon, 1977

Menaker, Daniel, *The Treatment*, New York: Washington Square Press, 1998

Miller, Michelle, *Hunger in the First Person Singular: Stories of Desire and Power*, Albuquerque: Amador Publishers, 1992

Mlodinow, Leonard, *Feynman's Rainbow: A Search for Beauty in Physics and in Life*, New York: Warner Books, 2003

Montaigne, de Michel, *The Complete Essays*, New York: Penguin Books, 1987

Mood, John J.L., Translator, *Rilke on Love and Other Difficulties*, New York: W.W. Norton & Company, 1975

Myss, Caroline, *Anatomy of the Spirit*, New York: Three Rivers Press, 1996

Newberg, Andrew, *Why God Won't Go Away*, New York: Ballantine Publishing Group, 2001

Nisker, Wes, *Buddha's Nature: A Practical Guide to Discovering Your Place in the Cosmos*, New York: Bantam Books, 2000

Nuland, Sherwin B., *How We Die*, New York: Vintage Books, 1995

Nyberg, David, *The Varnished Truth: Truth Telling and Deceiving in Ordinary Life*, Chicago: University of Chicago Press, 1993

Oates, David John, *Reverse Speech: Hidden Messages in Human Communication*, Indianapolis, IN: Knowledge Systems Inc., 1991

Palmer, Helen, *The Enneagram: Understanding Yourself and the Others in Your Life*, New York: HarperCollins, 1991

Peat, David F., *Synchronicity: The Bridge Between Matter and Mind*, New York: Bantam Books, 1987

Peck, M. Scott, *The Different Drum: Community Making and Peace*, New York: Simon & Schuster, 1987

--------------, *The Road Less Traveled: A New Psychology of Love, Traditional Values and Spiritual Growth*, New York: Simon & Schuster, 1978

--------------, *Further Along the Road Less Traveled: The Unending Journey Toward Spiritual Growth*, New York: Simon & Schuster, 1993

--------------, *People of the Lie: The Hope for Healing Human Evil*, New York: Simon & Schuster, 1983

--------------, *A World Waiting to be Born: Civility Rediscovered*, New York: Bantam Books, 1993

--------------, *A Bed by the Window: A novel of Mystery and Redemption*, New York: Bantam Books, 1990

--------------, *In Search of Stones: A Pilgrimage of Faith, Reason and Discovery*, New York: Hyperion, 1995

--------------, *In and Out of the Garbage Pail*, Moab, UT: Real Peoples Press, 1969

Pirsig, Robert M., *Lila: An Inquiry into Morals*, New York: Bantam Books, 1991

Quinn, Daniel, *The Story of B: An Adventure of Mind and Spirit*, New York: Bantam Books, 1996

--------------, *Ishmael*, New York: Bantam Books, 1993

Reich, Wilhelm, *Character Analysis*, New York: The Noonday Press, 1997

Reynolds, David K., *A Thousand Waves: A Sensible Life Style for Sensitive People*, New York: Quill, 1990

Roberts, Monty, *The Man Who Listens to Horses*, New York: Random House, 1997

Ruiz, Don Miguel, *The Four Agreements: A Toltec Wisdom Book*, San Rafael, CA Amber-Allen Publishing, 1997

Schiffer, Fredric, *Of Two Minds: The Revolutionary Science of Dual-Brain Psychology*, New York: The Free Press, 1998

Schnarch, David, *Passionate Marriage: Keeping Love & Intimacy Alive in Committed Relationships*, New York: Henry Holt and Company, 1998

Schwartz, Jeffrey M., *Brain Lock: Free Yourself from Obsessive-Compulsive Behavior*, New York: Regan Books/HarperCollins, 1996

Scott, Susan, *Fierce Conversations: Achieving Success at Work & in Life, One Converstaion at a Time*, New York: Viking, 2002

Shlain, Leonard, *The Alphabet Versus the Goddess: The Conflict Between Word and Image*, New York: Viking, 1998

Sturgeon, Theodore, *More Than Human*, New York: Vintage Books, 1999

--------------, *Venus Plus X*, New York: Vintage Books, 1999

--------------, Theodore, *Godbody*, New York: Donald I. Fine, 1986

--------------, Theodore, *The Ultimate Egoist*, Berkeley: North Atlantic Books, 1994

Talbot, Michael, *The Holographic Universe*, New York: HarperCollins, 1991

Torrey, E. Fuller, *The Death of Psychiatry*, Radnor, PA: Chilton Book Company, 1974

Villasenor, Daniel, *The Lake*, New York: Penguin Books, 2000

Watts, Alan, *The Way of Zen*, New York: Vintage Books, 1957

--------------, *The Book on the Taboo Against Knowing Who You Are*, New York: Vintage Books, 1966

--------------, *Zen Effects: The Life of Alan Watts*, Woodstock, VT: Skylight Paths Publishing, 2001

--------------, *The Wisdom of Insecurity: A Message for an Age of Anxiety*, New York: Pantheon Books, 1951

--------------, *Psychotherapy East and West*, New York: Vintage Books, 1961

--------------, *The Two Hands of God:*, Macmillan Publishing, 1963

--------------, *Still the Mind: An Introduction to Meditation*, Novato, CA New World Library, 2000

Wegner, Daniel and Pennebaker, James W., Editors. *Handbook of Mental Control*, Englewood Cliffs, NJ: Prentice-Hall, Inc., 1993

Weil, Andrew, *The Natural Mind: An Investigation of Drugs and the Higher Consciousness*, Boston: HoughtonMifflin Company, 1972

Welwood, John, *Toward a Psychology of Awakening: Buddhism, Psychotherapy, and the Path of Personal and Spiritual Transformation*, Boston: Shambhala Publications, Inc., 2000

White, Lancelot law, *The Next Development in Man*, New York: Henry Holt and Company, 1948

Wilber, Ken, *A Brief History of Everything*, Boston: Shambhala Publications, Inc., 2000

--------------, *Grace and Grit: Spirituality and Healing in the Life and Death of Treya Killam Wilber*, Boston: Shambhala Publications, Inc., 2000

--------------, *Boomeritis: A Novel that Will Set You Free*, Boston: Shambhala Publications, Inc., 2002

--------------, *Thought as Passion*, Albany: State University of New York Press, 2003

--------------, *No Boundary: Eastern and Western Approaches to personal Growth*, Boston Shambhala Publications, Inc., 2001

--------------, *One Taste: Daily Reflections on Integral Spirituality*, Boston: Shambhala Publications, Inc., 2000

Wilson, Edward O., *Consilience: The Unity of Knowledge*, New York: Vintage Books, 1999

Wilson, Robert Anton, *Prometheus Rising*, Tempe, AZ: New Falcon Publications, 1994

Wolff, Dina, Editor, *The Autobiography of Robert Jay Wolff: The Man From Highbelow*, Durango, CO: Authentic Publishing, 2001

Woodward, Bob, *Maestro: Greenspan's Fed and the American Boom*, New York: Simon & Schuster, 2000

Wright, Robert, *The Moral Animal: Evolutionary Psychology and Everyday Life*, New York: Vintage Books, 1995

Yalom, Irvin D., *Momma and the Meaning of Life: Tales of Psychotherapy*, New York: Perennial, 2000

--------------, *Love's Executioner: Other Tales of Psychotherapy*, New York: Perennial, 2000

--------------, *Lying on the Couch*, New York: HarperCollins, 1997

--------------, *Every Day Gets A Little Closer*, New York: Basic Books, 1974

--------------, *Existential Psychotherapy*, New York: Basic Books, 1980

--------------, *When Nietzsche Wept*, New York: HarperCollins, 1992

--------------, *The Schopenhauer Cure*, New York: HarperCollins, 2005

Next Steps . . .

*A Way For
You To
Give Back*   →   Did you help yourself with my book?
If so, please write a brief review at:
www.Amazon.com

*To Change
Your Life*   →   Change that comes easy doesn't last and lasting change doesn't come easy. If you really want to change your life, come immerse yourself in one of our week-long retreats.

*To Earn
CEU's*   →   If you are a therapist or counselor interested in exploring new ways of working with clients, we offer CEU's.

*To Get
Certified*   →   If you're interested in becoming certified to teach Reology—look into our trainer's training.

*To Ask
Questions*   →   If you have a personal question, send me an email and I'll send you a personalized response with suggestions.

For More Information:

<u>Write</u>
The Reology Institute
PO Box 817
Tesuque, NM 87574

<u>Visit</u>
www.Reology.org

<u>Email</u>
Jake@Reology.org

CPSIA information can be obtained
at www.ICGtesting.com
Printed in the USA
FSOW04n0007300616
22195FS